Fundamental Rights

BOOKS BY MILTON R. KONVITZ

Author

On the Nature of Value

The Alien and the Asiatic in American Law

The Constitution and Civil Rights

Civil Rights in Immigration

Fundamental Liberties of a Free People: Religion, Speech, Press, Assembly

A Century of Civil Rights

Expanding Liberties

Religious Liberty and Conscience

Judaism and the American Idea

Torah and Constitution: Essays in American Jewish Thought

Nine American Jewish Thinkers

Fundamental Rights: History of a Constitutional Doctrine

Editor

Bill of Rights Reader: Leading Constitutional Cases

First Amendment Freedoms: Selected Cases on Freedom of Religion, Speech, Press, Assembly

Judaism and Human Rights

The Recognition of Ralph Waldo Emerson

Emerson: A Collection of Critical Essays (With Stephen E. Whicher)

The American Pragmatists (with Gail Kennedy)

Freedom and Experience (with Sidney Hook)

Essays in Political Theory (with Arthur H. Murphy)

Aspects of Liberty (with Clinton Rossiter)

Law and Social Action: Selected Essays of Alexander H. Pekelis

Education for Freedom and Responsibility by Edmund Ezra Day

Liberian Code of Laws; Liberian Code of Laws Revised; Liberian Law Reports

Fundamental Rights

History of a
Constitutional Doctrine

Milton R. Konvitz

Transaction Publishers/Rutgers University
New Brunswick (U.S.A.) and London (U.K.)

Library of Congress Catalog Number: 00-059928
ISBN: 0-7658-0041-1
Printed in the United States of America

Library of Congress Cataloging-in-Publication Data

Konvitz, Milton Ridvas, 1908-
    Fundamental rights : history of a constitutional doctrine / Milton R. Konvitz
        p. cm.
    Includes bibliographical references.
    ISBN 0-7658-0041-1 (alk. paper)
    1. Civil rights—United States—History. I. Title.

    KF4749 .K633 2000
    342.73' 085—dc21   00-059928

For Josef

my son, who maketh a glad father

Proverbs 10:1

Contents

Preface

The twentieth century has been witness to many significant, even radical developments in American constitutional law. There was the "court-packing bill" sent by President Franklin D. Roosevelt to Congress in February 1937, there were the New Deal decisions of the Supreme Court that brought to an end the *Lochner* era, there was the Warren Court and the decisions that outlawed racial segregation, there were the Court decisions that established the principle of "one person, one vote." There was the decision that made privacy a constitutionally protected right. There was the decision that outlawed severely restrictive abortion laws. There were the decisions that virtually brought to an end censorship of literature, the stage, and the cinema. There was the case that made separation of church and state a constitutional principle. And there were others. When, however, the constitutional scholar looks at the forest rather than at the trees, he or she sees that the most significant and enduring development has been the extension of the Bill of Rights to the States, the so-called "incorporation" of the most important guarantees of the first eight amendments into the Due Process Clause of the Fourteenth Amendment, and the doctrine that there are rights that are so "fundamental" that any restriction is subject to judicial "strict scrutiny." The process has nationalized fundamental rights and has given these rights a preferred dignity and majesty.

This book attempts to tell the story of how fundamental rights have come into the United States Constitution. The development has been a slow and difficult process. It began in the early days of American jurisprudence, long before there was a Fourteenth Amendment, long before the Supreme Court became aware that there was a Due Process Clause. It was only slowly and only step-by-step that the Supreme Court gave life to the term "'liberty" as the word is used in the constitutional phrase "life, liberty and property."

As far as I know, the detailed history of this constitutional development has not been heretofore told. I think that it is eminently worth telling. The historical record brings to the fore the names of some Supreme Court Justices who have suffered an unmerited oblivion, as well as some that are prominent and honored.

The reader will find that there are some repetitions in the book, some cases are mentioned in different chapters, and a few passages are repeated, but this is due to the fact that the same authorities figure in diverse contexts, stand for different propositions. The repetitions are, therefore, intentional and purposeful.

The first chapter is introductory and also may serve as a helpful summary intended to provide a frame within which the following chapters may be more easily read. "A man," Dr. Johnson said to Boswell, "will turn over half a library to make one book"; so, too, a man may turn over half a book to make his first chapter.

1

The Idea of *Fundamental* Rights: Is There a Hierarchy of Constitutional Rights and Liberties?

In the famous second Flag Salute Case[1] the Supreme Court held that children of Jehovah's Witnesses, who believed that saluting the flag was a violation of the first of the Ten Commandments, could not constitutionally be compelled to participate in a daily flag salute ceremony at school, required by an act of the West Virginia Legislature. The decision was put on the broad ground that the compulsory flag salute was an invasion of the sphere of intellect and spirit—a sphere protected by the First and Fourteenth Amendments. National unity and patriotism may be fostered by persuasion and example, but there may be no coerced uniformity. Justice Felix Frankfurter, in an impassioned opinion, dissented. The legislation, he said, may be unwise, but the remedy for that should be in the legislature and not in the courts. Much legislation affecting freedom of thought and speech, he said, "should offend a free-spirited society" and is yet constitutional. The Court, he argued, has no constitutional power to give more weight or dignity, to place a higher value, on some rights guaranteed by the Bill of Rights than on others. There is nothing in the Constitution that gives the Court authority to be a more zealous guardian of some rights rather than of some others. "Our power," he said, does not vary according to the particular provision of the Bill of Rights which is invoked. The right not to have property taken without just compensation, has, so far as the scope of judicial power is concerned, the same constitutional dignity as the right to be protected against unreasonable searches and seizures, and the latter has no less claim than freedom of the press or freedom of speech or religious freedom.

Each specific right or liberty guaranteed by the Constitution must be, said Frankfurter, "equally respected," and the function of the Court "does not differ in passing on the constitutionality of legislation challenged under different Amendments."

The judicial history of the half-century since Justice Frankfurter wrote his dissenting opinion is that Frankfurter sadly misdirected his remarkably keen intellect and capacious eloquence. American constitutional law recognizes that, indeed, some rights and liberties enjoy more dignity than others, that some have a higher rank than others and deserve a greater degree of vigilance and protection than do others. I wish to show that this development is philosophically and jurisprudentially justified, and that its roots go further back than the New Deal or the Warren Court.

I.

In the theophany scene at Sinai, the Israelites heard the Ten Commandments.[2] The five commandments that are directed to relations between person and person are not listed in any special order of ranking in importance. One commandment simply follows another. Yet would anyone argue that the eighth commandment, "Neither shall you steal," is equal in importance to the sixth commandment, "You shall not kill"?

Although as formulated and promulgated, all five commandments appear to have equal status, the Mosaic legislation in fact does not treat them as equals, witness the fact that the punishment for murder is death, while for theft of property the penalty is restitution.[3] Obviously, there is in the Mosaic code of laws an implied hierarchy of values—life is more important than property, though this fact cannot be adduced from a mere reading of the Ten Commandments in isolation from the rest of the Pentateuch.

Indeed, as soon as a reflective mind faces a large body of legal enactments, or religious precepts, or moral maxims, or the world of phenomena, it feels compelled to organize them, to bring them into some order in which first things come first. Thus, e. g., we find in the Mishna (the authoritative code of rabbinic enactments from the 3rd century B. C. E. to the 3rd century C. E.) a formulation of the three beliefs that are to be considered basic in Judaism; namely, the existence of God, revelation, and a belief in retribution after death.[4] When the ancient rabbis considered the vast array of moral prohibitions, they selected three as the most important of all; namely, idolatry (which they associated with immoral pagan practices), incest (or adultery), and murder, and provided that one must not commit any one of these transgressions even under threat of death.[5] When they considered which moral laws ought to be held fundamental for all mankind (pagans or Jews, men or women), they listed seven commandments which they called the Seven Laws revealed to the descendants of Noah, the Noahide Laws.[6]

The leading philosophers and theologians of Judaism concerned themselves with this problem of fundamental laws, principles or doctrines. Philo of Alexandria (20 B. C. E.–50 C. E.) found that there are eight principles that are essential for Judaism.[7] In the Middle Ages, Maimonides (1135–1204) found thirteen articles of faith which he considered the "roots" or the "fundamentals"—the *ikkarim* or *yesodot*—of the religion.[8] Hasdai Crescas (1340–1410) had a more elaborate schema. He held that Judaism has three root principles, below which are six fundamentals of the faith. Then there are eight true beliefs, which are fundamental but not indispensable, and finally there are three true beliefs that are related to specific commandments.[9] Joseph Albo (1380–1444), in his work with the significant title *Sefer ha-Ikkarim* (*Book of Principles*), found only three root principles, from which flow derivative roots, and of an inferior order are six beliefs or *emunot*.[10]

Because Christianity needed to differentiate and separate itself from Judaism, and because it aggressively sought out proselytes, it early in its career placed heavy emphasis on creed, dogma, articles of faith, that would define orthodoxy and reduce the attractiveness of heresies. An encyclopedic survey of public confessions which have been or still were authoritative in various sections of the Christian Church in 1928 found that they exceeded 150![11] Perhaps the earliest was the Old Roman Creed (c. 100), that consisted of only twelve articles. In the third century came the Creed of Antioch. In the same century there was also the Creed of the Didascalia. In the fourth century the Nicene Council produced the Nicene Creed. The seventh century saw the promulgation of the Athanasian Creed. Looking back over the history of the great creeds, "one is amazed at the comparative simplicity of the great truths thus singled out by the common sense of the Church, through the centuries, as of primary importance."[12]

This is precisely the point that interests us: the search for and singling out what is of prime importance—the truths or values that are indispensable, that are the foundation stones of the superstructure; that there is an order among ideas, and a ranking among them.

II.

The impulse, both speculative and practical, that drives a thinker to seek the basic, fundamental elements of any reality can be clearly seen in the development of pre-Socratic philosophy or science. As Aristotle understood their teachings as they had been transmitted to him, the question that the early Ionian philosophers asked was: What is the basic stuff of which the world is composed?[13] They endeavored to find the answer in a single principle that would account for all qualities and all changes. Thales assumed that the fundamental principle is water. Anaximenes thought that the primary substance is air. The Pythagoreans asserted that numbers are the primary causes of things. Heraclitus taught that fire is the basic principle of substance. Leucippus and Democritus taught that numberless atoms are the fundamental stuff of which the world is made.[14]

The urge or incentive that drove the ancient philosophers to seek the elements fundamental to all reality is one that contemporary scientists share with their intellectual forebears. This drive for metaphysical or scientific fundamentals is not essentially different from the compulsion felt by theologians to formulate the essentials or primary, fundamental beliefs of a religious faith. And what compels theologians, metaphysicians, philosophers and scientists to seek fundamental truths also drives moral philosophers to try to formulate the fundamental moral qualities of man.

Thus, in classical Greek moral philosophy, as Plato implies in the *Republic*, four virtues were thought to be fundamental; namely, wisdom, courage, temperance, and justice. Plato adopted these virtues as comprising the essence of morality, as the primary qualities of virtue, which is the health of the soul. The Stoics adopted the Platonic canon of the four cardinal virtues, and made them the center of their teaching. (Cicero in *De Officiis* became for the Renaissance a prime source of the knowledge of the Platonic/Stoic virtues.) Early Greek and Latin Fathers of the Catholic Church adopted these pagan doctrines and gave them a Christian habitation and a name by attaching them to the Pauline triad of faith, hope, and charity. The result was that in time the Church taught that there are seven chief virtues: the four cardinal virtues that were known to pagans and that were now labeled as "natural," and the three preached by Paul and claimed to be "supernatural." Thomas Aquinas, however, adopted and assimilated the cardinal "natural" virtues and spoke of them, too, as supernatural, derived from the divine gifts of love.[15]

III.

From this brief review of the history of ideas in theology, philosophy, morality, and science it should be clear that a disciplined mind is forced to try to penetrate through a complex mass of ideas in order to reach concepts or propositions that point up the essential character of the mass of facts or ideas, disclosing what is relevant and what is irrelevant, what is important and what is only marginal, what is indispensable and what can be rejected. Indeed, as Socrates, Plato, and Aristotle contended, this is the very nature of conceptualization or thought, for a concept is an idea of something formed by mentally combining those characteristics that distinguish it from other things. This is the mental, intellectual process whether we try to define chair, ant, man, or, say, Christianity, virtue or goodness. As the process of conceptualization becomes more complex, as we try to reach the essential nature of, e. g., Judaism or Christianity, we feel compelled to find the root ideas without which other ideas would not follow, ideas that are basic as a foundation is basic to a house, a basic principle that serves as the groundwork on which the superstructure can be erected, or the primary idea from which other ideas can be deduced.

As used in the law, however, the term "fundamental" does not always have a precise meaning. It is at times used in an honorific sense, to underscore the importance of the idea or value in question, and it may suffice for the purpose and in the context in which it is used. It may contribute some intelligibility to a classification, it may make some decisions more predictable; it may help bring decisions or principles into a larger order of consistency. It may be used, not to describe or explain, but to guide conduct. It may express a wish or hope.[16]

In any case, we should bear in mind the wise counsel of Aristotle, that in studying this subject, we must be content if we attain "as high degree of certainty as the matter of it admits. The same accuracy or finish is not to be looked for in all discussions any more than in all the productions of the studio and workshop."[17] Besides, as William James noted, there is something to be said in favor of the vague, the imprecise, the indefinite.

IV.

When we turn to a consideration of the Bill of Rights of the United States Constitution, we are at once faced with the identical problem that we saw as we looked at the Ten Commandments. The First Amendment guarantees freedom of speech, press, assembly, religion, and petition. The Seventh Amendment provides that in civil suits, where the value in controversy exceeds twenty dollars, the right of trial by jury shall be preserved. Are these guarantees of equal dignity and worth? Despite the eloquent argument in Frankfurter's dissenting opinion in the second Flag Salute Case, I submit that they are no more of equal worth than are the prohibition on murder and on theft in the Ten Commandments. Yet the Bill of Rights makes no distinction between them. It became the task of the Supreme Court to classify the rights and liberties that are constitutionally guaranteed and place them in some reasonable order of dignity; and the process of sifting, weighing, and measuring them is an on-going and never-ending process. For values are always being reconsidered as new values arise and clamor for recognition, though the wording of the Bill of Rights remains *largely* unchanged.

It is not only that the rights guaranteed by the Constitution are subject to careful sifting and ordering, but, it is important to note, also that the Bill of Rights is itself the result of such a process—a process that began early in the Colonial period.

The pioneers to America's shores insisted on having written, binding charters and covenants that would guarantee them perpetual and unchangeable civil liberties. They insisted on having, in writing, guarantees of the writ of habeas corpus, trial by jury, right of counsel, a prohibition against excessive bail, the privilege against self-incrimination, freedom of speech and press, and a substantial measure of religious liberty. As early as 1639 the General Assembly of colonial Maryland adopted what it significantly called the "Act for the Liberties of the people," that reinforced the charter of 1632 and declared that all Christians in the colony

> Shall have and enjoy all such rights liberties immunities privileges and free customs . . . as any naturall born subject of England hath or ought to have or enjoy.[18]

In 1641 Nathaniel Ward drafted for the Massachusetts Bay Colony what was called the Body of Liberties—virtually a Bill of Rights. It provided that every person in the colony, inhabitant or foreigner, was entitled to equal protection of the law; that freemen had the right of petition; that an accused person was protected by the writ of habeas corpus; that "inhumane Barbarous or cruel" punishment was prohibited; that an accused person was permitted to have counsel; that husbands were prohibited from inflicting on their wives "bodilie correction or stripes" (unless administered in self-defense should she assault him); and it expressly recognized the right of emigration.[19] By the end of the seventeenth century there were charters of rights and liberties in at least seven of the thirteen American colonies.[20]

When the colonies had become independent sovereign states, following the Declaration of Independence in 1776, Virginia became the first state to adopt a written constitution and a Declaration of Rights—the latter drafted by George Mason—and by 1784 seven states had followed the example set by Virginia, and the remaining five states provided for the substance of personal liberty in the main body of their constitutions.[21]

Because of this panoply of guarantees of civil liberty by the states themselves, there was no groundswell of sentiment for a bill of rights at the Constitutional Convention. There was no felt need for it. In addition, there was the argument that since the Federal Government would have only specific, enumerated rights or powers, and all other rights or powers would be retained by the states or the people, there was no need to provide that the new government should not have certain powers, e. g., should have no power to curtail religious liberty or freedom of the press. Still, there were important leaders—Thomas Jefferson, George Mason, Eldridge Gerry, James Madison—who contended that a bill of rights was advisable, if not indispensable; and state conventions called to ratify the Constitution clamored for amendments that would constitute a bill of rights, and some of the state conventions even made specific proposals.[22] In all, 124 amendments were submitted by the states.[23] In the first Congress, Madison introduced eight resolutions, only five of which were relevant to a bill of rights. The House of Representatives adopted seventeen proposals; the senate rejected two and consolidated the remainder to twelve, and these were accepted by the House and were submitted to the states, which ratified only ten, which have come to be known as the Bill of Rights.[24]

A point to be noted is that the process of deciding what rights and liberties are fundamental, indispensable, and which ones may be important but are not imperative, was not begun by the Supreme Court. The process has a long history that can be traced back to the early years of the American colonies, and even back to the Mayflower Compact of 1620, by which the Pilgrims covenanted to enact only "just and equal laws, Ordinances, Acts, Constitutions, and Offices."[25] Madison, who was mainly responsible for the framing and enactment of the Bill of Rights, spoke of "the great rights, the trial by jury, freedom of the press, . . . liberty of conscience." He did not speak in such superlative terms of other guarantees, although willing to provide for them in the amendments.[26]

V.

The first attempt by a Justice of the Supreme Court to formulate explicitly the idea of fundamental rights was made in 1823, thirty-four years after the United States Constitution was ratified. Justice Bushrod Washington, sitting on circuit, had before him the case of *Corfield* v. *Coryell*,[27] that involved the question whether the State of New Jersey was constitutionally required to allow citizens of other states to gather shellfish in its waters. Article IV, Section 2, of the Constitution has a Privileges and Immunities Clause that provides that "[the] citizens of each State shall be entitled to all the privileges and immunities of citizens in the several States." "The inquiry is," wrote Justice Washington, what are the privileges and immunities of citizens in the several States? We feel no hesitation in confining these expressions to those privileges and immunities which are, in their nature, fundamental; which belong, of right, to the citizens of all free governments; and which have, at all times, been enjoyed by the citizens of the several States which compose this Union, . . . "

Justice Washington then specified the following rights as "fundamental" within the above description:

protection by the government;

"the enjoyment of life and liberty, with the right to acquire and possess property of every kind, and to pursue and obtain happiness and safety";

the right of a citizen of one State to pass through or to reside in any other State, for purposes of trade, agriculture, professional pursuits, or otherwise;

the benefits of the writ of habeas corpus;

to institute or maintain actions in the courts of the State;

to take, hold and dispose of property;

exemption from higher taxes than those paid by other citizens of the State.

At the time Justice Washington wrote his opinion, the Natural Law-Natural Rights theory was widely held, by some Justices of the Supreme Court, some members of Congress, and leading abolitionists.[28] And it has been responsibly said:

If it had been accepted by the Court, this theory [as formulated by Justice Washington] might well have endowed the Supreme Court with a reviewing power over restrictive state legislation as broad as that which it later came to exercise under the due process and equal protection clauses of the Fourteenth Amendment, but it was firmly rejected by the Court.[29]

The list of rights designated as "fundamental" by Justice Washington fails to mention rights which today come readily to mind, such as religious liberty, freedom of speech and press. One reason for the omission is that he was deciding a case in 1823, more than a century before the Court had begun to make applicable to the states the rights guaranteed by the Bill of Rights. Secondly, Justice Washington concentrated his thoughts on the rights that he considered to be inherent in the concept of citizenship in a democratic country, "those privileges and immunities which are, in their nature, fundamental; which belong, of right, to the citizens of all free governments." In any case, it is noteworthy that, in addition to citing some examples of what he considered to be fundamental—specific rights,—he resorted to the Declaration of Independence to say that citizens have the fundamental right to "the enjoyment of life and liberty, . . . and to pursue and obtain happiness and safety." He thus used the broadest possible terms, words into which one may be free to read specific rights essential to life, liberty, and happiness, like those enumerated in the Bill of Rights and even more. Justice Bushrod Washington thus deserves honor for being the first Supreme Court Justice to open up the inquiry into the subject of fundamental rights—rights which are, "in their nature, fundamental; which belong, of right, to the citizens [only we would today say "people"] of all free governments." This is no small honor.

VI.

Although Justice Bushrod Washington was the first Justice of the Supreme Court to single out certain rights and liberties—or certain privileges and immunities—as fundamental, it was James Madison who first singled out certain rights as being preeminently important, while certain others, though essential, were not to be thought of as "natural rights."

On June 8, 1789, Madison moved in the first Congress of the United States that a select committee be appointed to consider and report on amendments to the Constitution. Then he proceeded to speak about eight amendments that he would sponsor. Of these, five proposals contained what were to become the Bill of Rights. In the course of his presentation he had occasion to mention "the three great rights, the trial by jury, freedom of the press, or liberty of conscience. . . . " These, to Madison, were the most important, the most basic, the most highly prized rights or liberties. Then he said that the "freedom of the press and rights of conscience, those choicest privileges of the people," though unguarded in the British Constitution, must be safeguarded by the U. S. Constitution. Madison then divided bills of rights into five categories, of which only the following two are relevant for our purpose:

3. Those specifying the rights retained by the people when particular powers are given up to be exercised by the Legislature.
4. Those that seem to result from the nature of the social compact, such as trial by jury, which cannot be considered as a natural right yet is no less essential to securing the liberty of the people.

Commenting on this presentation by Madison, Irving Brant, author of the six-volume biography of Madison, wrote:

> The position Madison took might be called "the doctrine of the pre-eminence of the great rights." It furnishes a complete refutation, dated 1789, of the contention sometimes . . . made that all guarantees of the Bill of Rights are on an exact parity with each other in constitutional importance and enforceability. This tends to the conclusion that there is no more forcefulness to the words, "Congress shall make no law abridging the freedom of the press," than to the clause preserving jury trial in civil suits involving more than $20.00. This makes it easier to strip away the mandatory quality of the First Amendment and to leave the great freedoms subject to any abridgment that does not shock five members of the Supreme Court.[30]

VII.

When the first Congress adopted the amendments to the Constitution, and the States ratified them, and they became the Bill of Rights, it was clearly understood that these amendments would be guarantees only against actions by Congress and the Federal Government. The Bill of Rights was not intended to be a limitation on actions by the States. In 1833 the Supreme Court judicially affirmed this understanding.[31] The possibility of a change came after the Civil War with the adoption of the Fourteenth Amendment (1868), that included the Due Process Clause: "nor shall any State deprive any person of life, liberty, or property, without due process of law," and the Equal Protection Clause: "nor deny to any person within its jurisdiction the equal protection of the laws." For the first century and a half, however, as far as the Supreme Court was concerned, the constitutional guarantees hardly existed. In his study of this subject published in 1943, the eminent scholar of constitutional law Henry Steele Commager reached the following conclusions:

1. There were very few instances where the Congress threatened the integrity of the constitutional system or the guarantees of the Bill of Rights.
2. As far as concerned federal legislation in the few instances that affected personal liberties, the judicial record was practically barren. The record "discloses not a single case, in a century and a half, where the Supreme Court has protected freedom of speech, press, assembly, or petition against congressional attack."
3. The record "reveals no instance [with one possible exception] where the court has intervened on behalf of the underprivileged—the Negro, the alien, women, children, workers, tenant-farmers. It reveals, on the

contrary, that the court has effectively intervened again and again to defeat congressional efforts to free slaves, guarantee civil rights to Negroes, to protect workingmen, outlaw child labor, assist hard-pressed farmers, and to democratize the tax system. From this analysis the Congress, and not the courts, emerges as the instrument for the realization of the guarantees of the bill of rights.[32]

There were, fortunately, voices of protest in the Supreme Court, members of the Court who sought to put life into the Bill of Rights and into the Due Process and Equal Protection Clauses of the Fourteenth Amendment, most notably the first Justice John M. Harlan, and Justices Oliver Wendell Holmes, Louis D. Brandeis, Edward T. Sanford, Charles Evans Hughes, Benjamin N. Cardozo, and Harlan F. Stone.

Justice Harlan, in cases before the Court in 1884 and in 1908,[33] argued, in dissenting opinions, that the procedural guarantees provided in the Bill of Rights as applicable to crimes against Federal law should be equally applicable to crimes against State law, under the Due Process Clause of the Fourteenth Amendment.

It was not, however, until 1925 that the Supreme Court for the first time held a guarantee of the Bill of Rights to be applicable to the States under the Due Process Clause of the Fourteenth Amendment. In the landmark case of *Gitlow* v. *New York*,[34] in an opinion by Justice Sanford, the Court held that "freedom of speech and of the press . . . are among the fundamental personal rights and liberties protected by the due process clause of the Fourteenth Amendment from impairment by the States." This decision marked the beginning of the process that sometimes came to be called "incorporation" of a provision of the Bill of Rights into the Due Process Clause of the Fourteenth Amendment.

In 1931, six years later, the Court had before it the conviction of a person for violating the California law that prohibited the public display of a red flag. The Court, in *Stromberg* v. *California*,[35] in an opinion by Chief Justice Hughes, held the California Red Flag Law unconstitutional as a violation of the "liberty" protected by the Fourteenth Amendment. This was the first time that the Court declared a State statute unconstitutional on First Amendment free speech grounds.[36]

It was not, however, until 1937 that the Court, for the first time, formulated a doctrine of fundamental rights, under which rights and liberties guaranteed by the Bill of Rights and other rights as well, could be tested, and accepted or rejected as fundamental. If fundamental, then they could be read into the concept of "liberty" as this term is used in the Due Process Clause of the Fourteenth Amendment, and therefore could be enforced as a constitutional guarantee against the States.

Palko v. *Connecticut*[37] involved a claim by the defendant that he had been subjected to double jeopardy by the State of Connecticut. Now, if he had been a defendant in a Federal case, he could have claimed the protection of the Double Jeopardy guarantee of the Fifth Amendment. The Court rejected the defendant's argument that the guarantee was "incorporated" into the Due Process Clause of the Fourteenth Amendment. Why? Because, wrote Justice Cardozo for the Court, it was not a fundamental right. What are fundamental rights? Justice Cardozo stated a principle or doctrine that has served as a standard or test, words that have become among the most famous in the Supreme Court's jurisprudence. Those rights are fundamental, wrote Justice Cardozo, that

> represented the very essence of a scheme of ordered liberty . . . principles of justice so rooted in the traditions and conscience of our people as to be ranked as fundamental.

Freedom of speech and the press, said Justice Cardozo, meet the test of fundamental rights. "If the Fourteenth Amendment has absorbed them, the process of absorption has had its source in the belief that neither liberty nor justice would exist if they were sacrificed." Of freedom of thought and speech "one may say that it is the matrix, the indispensable condition, of nearly every other form of freedom." The test of a State's action is this: "Does it violate those 'fundamental principles of liberty and justice which lie at the base of all our civil and political institutions?'"

What Justice Cardozo accomplished with his opinion in *Palko* is the principle that the Constitution, through judicial interpretation, contains a hierarchy of values, some of which are recognized as "fundamental." By applying the *Palko* test or yardstick, the Court has held that some guarantees of the Bill of Rights are so fundamental that they must be held to be absorbed into the Due Process Clause of the Fourteenth Amendment and are binding on the States. In brief, the fundamental rights have been nationalized. The following rights enumerated in the Bill of Rights have not been made applicable to the States; that is, they have not been found to be fundamental:

The Second Amendment right to keep and bear arms;

The Third Amendment prohibiting quartering of soldiers in any house in time of peace;

The Fifth Amendment provision for indictment by a grand jury in cases involving capital or otherwise infamous crime;

The Seventh Amendment guarantee of trial by jury in civil cases;

The Eighth Amendment prohibition of excessive bail or fines.

These, on their face, can hardly be said to qualify for inclusion in any Honor Roll of fundamental rights and liberties.

While the principle of the Cardozo opinion in *Palko* may be said to have generally prevailed in subsequent decisions, thus firmly settling that there is indeed a hierarchy of constitutional guarantees, and that selective incorporation of some of the provisions of the Bill of Rights into the Due Process Clause of the Fourteenth Amendment has been achieved, the Cardozo philosophy and the judicial process that it has validated have had their opponents. The most notable protest was voiced by Justice Hugo Black in his dissenting opinion in *Adamson* v. *California*.[38] He argued that the adoption of the Fourteenth Amendment was historically intended to make fully applicable to the States each and every one of the first eight Amendments. Selective incorporation meant judicial usurpation. There was no historical or constitutional warrant, he contended, for the Court's practice of substituting its own notions of decency and fundamental justice, its own version of natural law and natural rights, for the language of the Bill of Rights.

Justices William O. Douglas, Frank Murphy, and Wiley B. Rutledge concurred with Justice Black's dissent, but the latter two expressed an important reservation. While they agreed that all of the specific guarantees of the Bill of Rights should be carried over intact into the Fourteenth Amendment, they were not prepared, they said, to say that the Fourteenth Amendment is entirely and necessarily limited to what is provided in the Bill of Rights.

This expressed misgiving, that the Black approach was unduly confining, at the same time that it was properly open and embracing, was prescient of what was to come.

A Connecticut statute of 1879 made it a crime for any person to use a contraceptive. Two members of the Planned Parenthood League of Connecticut—its executive director and medical director—were convicted of violating the statute by giving medical advice, information and instruction to married persons regarding use of contraceptives. In

Griswold v. *Connecticut* (1965) the Supreme Court held the statute unconstitutional as an infringement on the right to privacy of married persons. Such privacy, the Court held, is a fundamental personal right. Although privacy is not explicitly listed as one of the enumerated rights in the Constitution, Justice Douglas, in his opinion for the Court, said that "specific guarantees . . . have penumbras, formed by emanations from those guarantees that help give them life and substance." Just as freedom of association is implied in the guaranteed freedom of speech, so the right of privacy is generated by the First, Third, Fourth, Fifth, and Ninth Amendments.[39]

In a concurring opinion (in which Chief Justice Earl Warren and Justice William Brennan joined), Justice Arthur Goldberg, while finding merit in the penumbra and emanations argument of Justice Douglas, argued that "liberty [as guaranteed by the Fourteenth Amendment] protects those personal rights that are fundamental, and is not confined to the specific terms of the Bill of Rights." He conceded that the Fourteenth Amendment does not "incorporate" into the guarantee of liberty all of the first eight Amendments, however, the Ninth Amendment ("The enumeration in the Constitution of certain rights shall not be construed to deny or disparage others retained by the people"), by its language and history, provides strong support for the Court's incorporation of additional unenumerated rights that are "so rooted in the traditions and conscience of our people as to be ranked fundamental."

VIII.

We have noted that the first Justice Harlan deserves special recognition for arguing, in dissenting opinions, that the procedural safeguards of the Bill of Rights should be applied to the States as they are to the Federal Government, thus pointing to the fecundity of the Due Process Clause of the Fourteenth Amendment. Similarly, credit should be given to Justice Holmes. In his famous dissenting opinion in *Lochner* v. *New York*[40] he wrote:

> I think that the word liberty in the Fourteenth Amendment is perverted when it is held to prevent the natural outcome of a dominant opinion, unless it can be said that a rational and fair man necessarily would admit that the statute proposed would infringe *fundamental principles as they have been understood by the traditions of our people and our law.* (Italics supplied.)

For our interest at this point in this discussion, however, much more important is the contribution that Justice Holmes made to the judicial test that has come to be called "strict scrutiny." In *Abrams* v. *United States*,[41] a freedom of speech case that arose in the course of World War I, Justice Holmes, in a dissenting opinion in which he was joined by Justice Brandeis, contended that economic legislation needed only a rational basis to establish its constitutionality, but a limitation on freedom of speech can be justified only by proof of a "clear and present danger." The clearest articulation of the clear and present danger test was in a concurring opinion by Justice Brandeis, in which he was joined by Justice Holmes, in *Whitney* v. *California*,[42] decided in 1927, in which he wrote:

> Thus all fundamental rights comprised within the term liberty are protected by the Federal Constitution from invasion by the States. The right of free speech, the right to teach and the right of assembly are, of course, fundamental rights. . . . These may not be denied or abridged. But, although the rights of free speech and assembly are fundamental, they are not in their nature absolute. Their exercise is subject to restriction, if the particular restriction proposed is required in order to protect the State from destruction or from serious injury, political, economic, or moral. That the necessity which is essential to a valid restriction does not exist unless speech would produce, or is intended to produce, a clear and imminent danger of some substantial evil which the State constitutionally may seek to prevent has been settled.

It is important to note that the point of departure for Justices Brandeis and Holmes was not the Bill of Rights but the term "liberty" as it exists in the Due Process Clause. What does the term liberty mean? It means the fundamental rights. The Due Process Clause, then, protects all fundamental rights against invasion by the States. The right of free speech and the right of assembly are fundamental rights. Can a State ever restrict such rights, restrict a fundamental right? Yes, but only if the State can prove that the exercise of the fundamental right, in the circumstances, would create a clear and imminent or present danger to a substantial State interest, or would create a substantial evil which the State may constitutionally prevent from occurring.

Justice Brandeis, in short compass, formulated the basic operative constitutional principles that came to fruition in the following decades of the twentieth century. One of the principles has come to be known as "strict scrutiny." The clear and present danger test essentially meant that when a State restricts a fundamental right, its action is not presumed to be constitutional; on the contrary, it is presumed to be unconstitutional; it is subjected to the test of "strict scrutiny" by the Court, and the State is required to justify its action. It is this test of strict scrutiny that gives advantage to the fundamental rights as distinguished from claims that are not fundamental rights.

In the absence of strict scrutiny, the challenged governmental action is generally found to have been constitutional, but an action subjected to strict scrutiny has little chance of being upheld as constitutional. In one case it is sufficient if the State shows that its action "reasonably" relates to a "legitimate " governmental interest, in the other case, when the official action is subjected to the test of strict scrutiny, the government must show that it has a compelling interest.

The most frequently used formulation of this principle of strict scrutiny was written by Justice Stone in *United States* v. *Carolene Products Co.*,[43] in one of the most important footnotes in American jurisprudence. Citing cases involving restrictions on voting, speech and assembly, Justice Stone wrote that

> legislation which restricts those political processes which can ordinarily be expected to bring about repeal of undesirable legislation, [may] be subjected to more exacting judicial scrutiny . . . than are most other types of legislation . . . [And] similar considerations [may] enter into review of statutes directed at particular religious, . . . or national, . . . or racial minorities . . . prejudice against discrete and insular minorities may be a special condition, which tends seriously to curtail the operation of those political processes ordinarily to be relied upon to protect minorities, and which may call for a correspondingly more searching judicial inquiry. . . .

Thus the *Carolene* principle of a double-standard—the minimum scrutiny for economic and social legislation, and strict scrutiny for State actions that infringe fundamental rights and liberties—probably evolved from the Cardozo principle in *Palko,* which probably evolved from Brandeis's *Whitney* doctrine. In any case, what we have is settled constitutional doctrine that there is, indeed (and contrary to the teaching of Justices Frankfurter and Black), a hierarchy of rights, and that some rights must receive more vigilance and protection than others.

We began our discussion by showing that religions like Judaism and Christianity inevitably came in time to select certain beliefs as basic, fundamental characteristics that became known, generally, as dogmas. These, it is said, are so important that to deny them is to espouse heresy, to subvert the religion, to force the house to topple. In America's "civil religion," fundamental rights and liberties function as dogmas, for to deny them is to undo the "ordered liberty" that America represents.[44] The Declaration of Independence, the Constitution (especially the Bill of Rights and the Fourteenth Amendment with its Due Process and Equal Protection Clauses) are sacred scripture. "The God of the civil religion," it has been noted, is "much more related to order, law, and right than to salvation and love."[45] What expresses, orchestrates, and implements "order, law, and right" more than does the Constitution with the Supreme Court's emphasis on fundamental rights and liberties and their protection, their policing under the club of strict scrutiny?

Notes

1. *West Virginia State Board of Education* v. *Barnette*, 319 U.S. 624 (1943), overruling *Minersville School District* v. *Gobitis*, 310 U.S. 586 (1940).
2. Exodus 20; Deuteronomy 5.
3. Exodus 23; Numbers 35:16; Deuteronomy 4:41–43.
4. Mishnah, Sanhedrin 10:2.
5. Babylonian Talmud, Sanhedrin 74a.
6. *Ibid.*, at 56a.
7. Wolfson, Harry A., *Philo, Foundations of Religious Philosophy* (Cambridge, Mass., 1947), I, 164–165.
8. Maimonides, *Commentary on the Mishnah*. Helek Sanhedrin, ch. 10. Isadore Twersky, ed., *A Maimonides Reader* (New York, 1972), 417–423. Maimonides, *Guide of the Perplexed*, trans. S. Pines (Chicago, 1963), 435.
9. Haddai Crescas, *Or Adonai* (1410). Wolfson, Harry A., *Crescas' Critique of Aristotle* (Cambridge, Mass., 1929), 319, n. 1. Husik, I., *A History of Medieval Jewish Philosophy* (Philadelphia, 1916), 392, 402.
10. Joseph Albo, *Sefer Ha-Ikkarim. Book of Principles*, trans. I. Husik (Philadelphia, 1929), I, ch. 26.
11. *Encyclopedia of Religion and Ethics*, James Hastings, editor (New York, 1928), III, 831.
12. *Ibid.*, IV, 242.
13. Aristotle, *Metaphysics*, Bk. A, 3: 983b, 6–11; 984a, 2–7.
14. Thilly, Frank, *A History of Philosophy*. 3rd ed., rev. by Ledger Wood (New York, 1957), 20–51.
15. Edelstein, Ludwig, *The Meaning of Stoicism* (Cambridge, Mass., 1966), 90–91. See also op. cit. supra note 11, at vol. XI, 431–432; cf. Randall, John Herman, Jr., *Hellenistic Ways of Deliverance and the Making of the Christian Synthesis* (New York, 1970), 136–144.
16. Columbia Associates in Philosophy, *An Introduction to Reflective Thinking* (Boston, 1923), 336–337.
17. Aristotle, *Nichomachean Ethics*, Bk. I, ch. 3.
18. Rutland, R. A., *The Birth of the Bill of Rights* (Chapel Hill, 1955) , 14.
19. *Ibid.*, pp. 15–16.
20. *Ibid.*, ch. II.

21. *Ibid.*, pp. 76, 77.
22. Dumbauld, Edw., *The Bill of Rights and What It Means Today* (Norman, Okla., 1957), 3–33, 36.
23. Bernard Schwartz, The *Bill of Rights: a Documentary History* (New York, 1971), 2: 627–980.
24. Milton R. Konvitz, *Fundamental Liberties of a Free People* (Ithaca, NY., 1957), 345–361.
25. Commager, H. S., *Documents of American History* (New York, 8th ed., 1965), 15.
26. Brant, Irving, *The Bill of Rights, Its Origins and Meaning* (Indianapolis, 1965), 45.
27. *Corfield* v. *Coryell*, 6 Fed. Cas. 546 (No. 3230) (Circ. Ct. East. Dist. Pa.) (1823).
28. Benj. F. Fletcher, *American Interpretations of Natural Law* (Cambridge, Mass., 1931); Chas. Grove Haines, *The Revival of Natural Law Concepts* (Cambridge, Mass., 1930); C. G. Le Boutillier, *American Democracy and Natural Law* (New York, 1950).
29. *The Constitution of the United States*, Congressional Research Service, Library of Congress (Washington, D. C., 1987), 872; *McKane* v. *Durston*, 153 U.S. 684 (1894); *Chambers* v. *Baltimore & O. R. R.*, 207 U.S. 142 (1907); *Whitfield* v. *Ohio*, 297 U.S. 431 (1936). In *Baldwin* v. *Montana Fish and Game Comm.*, 436 U.S. 371 (1978), the Court said: "Only with respect to those 'privileges' and 'immunities' bearing upon the vitality of the Nation as a single entity must the State treat all citizens, resident and non-resident, equally." See also *Hicklin* v. *Orbeck*, 437 U.S. 518 (1978).
30. Op. cit. note 26 supra, at p. 47.
31. *Barron* v. *Baltimore*, 32 U.S. 243 (1833).
32. H. S. Commager, *Majority Rule and Minority Rights* (London, New York, 1943), 47, 55.
33. *Hurtado* v. *Calif.*, 110 U.S. 516 (1884); *Twining* v. *N. J.*, 211 U.S. 78 (1908).
34. *Gitlow* v. *New York*, 260 U.S. 652 (1925).
35. *Stromberg* v. *Calif.*, 283 U.S. 359 (1931).
36. Cf *Near* v. *Minn.*, 283 U.S. 697 (1931).
37. *Palko* v. *Conn.*, 302 U.S. 319 (1937). The specific holding of the case, that the double jeopardy guarantee is not applicable to the States, was overruled in *Benton* v. *Maryland*, 395 U.S. 784 (1969).
38. *Adamson* v. *Calif.*, 332 U.S. 46 (1947).
39. *Griswold* v. *Conn.*, 381 U.S. 479 (1965). In *Eisenstadt* v. *Baird*, 405 U.S. 438 (1972) the right of privacy was extended to unmarried persons who used contraceptives. In *Roe* v. *Wade*, 410 U.S. 113 (1973) the Court upheld the right to an abortion as a fundamental right of privacy.
40. *Lochner* v. *New York*, 198 U.S. 45 (1905).
41. *Abrams* v. *United States*, 250 U.S. 616 (1919).
42. *Whitney* v. *Calif.*, 274 U.S. 357 (1927).
43. *United States* v. *Carolene Products Co.*, 304 U.S. 144, n. 4 (1938).
44. Robert N. Bellah, "Civil Religion in America," in *American Civil Religion*, R. E. Richey and D. G. Jones, eds. (New York, 1974), 21, 30.
45. *Ibid.*, 231.

2

"Every Right and Privilege
Belonging to a Freeman"

I.

After *Corfield*[1] fifty years passed before there was another notable occasion for a judicial consideration of the question whether there were certain fundamental rights that were inherent in the concept of American citizenship.

The original United States Constitution contained no definition of American citizenship; and the *Dred Scott*[2] decision of 1857 held that free Negroes were not citizens and did not enjoy access to Federal courts. To overrule this decision, the Fourteenth Amendment defined citizenship by providing that "All persons born or naturalized in the United States . . . are citizens of the United States and of the State wherein they reside." Moving beyond the bestowal of citizenship on the Negro—and, by the Thirteenth Amendment, the abolition of slavery—the Congress that formulated the Civil War Amendments sought to make sure that the Negroes' rights as free men and citizens would not be merely empty promises, airy nothings; and so, immediately following the Citizenship Clause, the Fourteenth Amendment provided that "No State shall make or enforce any law which shall abridge the privileges or immunities of citizens of the United States."

John A. Bingham, principal draftsman of the Fourteenth Amendment, shared the views of Justice Washington with regard to the national character of privileges and immunities. The amendment, he said, would give Congress the power to protect by national law the privileges and immunities of all the citizens of the Republic, and the inborn rights of every person within its jurisdiction whenever the same shall be abridged or denied by the unconstitutional acts of any state . . . No state ever had the right, under the forms of law or otherwise, to deny to any free man the equal protection of the laws or to abridge the privileges or immunities of any citizen of the Republic. . . . [3]

Senator Jacob M. Howard, when he presented the Fourteenth Amendment to the Senate, maintained that the Privileges or Immunities Clause of Section 1 of the Amendment guaranteed to citizens of the United States the privileges and immunities secured by Article IV, Section 2—the so-called Comity Clause. For a list of such privileges and immunities of American citizens, Senator Howard turned to the opinion of Justice Washington in *Corfield*. "The great object of the first section of this amendment is, therefore," he said, "to restrain the power of the states and compel them at all times to respect these great fundamental guarantees."[4]

A leading historian of the origins of the Fourteenth Amendment has summarized his views of the intention of the Privileges or Immunities Clause:

The privileges or immunities . . . were the natural rights of all men. . . . They were the rights to life, liberty, and property. They were the rights to contract, and to own, use, and dispose of property. They were the rights to equal protection of the courts and to the full and equal protection of the laws. They were the rights of unrestricted travel, sojourn, and residence. . . .

The privileges or immunities clause was regarded [by its sponsors] as reenacting the comity clause of Article IV [Section 2] into which United States citizenship and natural rights had been read. It was a constitutional reaffirmation of a principle binding without constitutional mention, the reciprocal relationship of allegiance and protection. . . . [5]

In brief, the intention of the framers and proponents of the Privileges or Immunities Clause of the Fourteenth Amendment was to reaffirm the fundamental rights doctrine of Justice Washington; i.e., that American citizens have certain fundamental rights, which may not be denied or abridged by any State; and that by Section 5, Congress will have the power to enforce, by appropriate legislation, against the States, these privileges and immunities.

II.

Five years after the Fourteenth Amendment was ratified, the Supreme Court, in *Slaughter-House Cases*, in 1873, gave the Privileges or Immunities Clause so narrow a construction as to make it practically meaningless. As we shall see, however, the dissenting opinions contributed significantly to the development of the idea of fundamental rights in American constitutional thought. The greatest liar, Dr. Johnson said, tells more truth than falsehood; so it may be that the *Slaughter-House Cases*, from the perspective of a hundred years' history, perhaps stand for more good than evil.

The facts in these cases were these: A Louisiana statute chartered a private corporation and vested in it the exclusive right to establish and maintain stockyards and slaughterhouses in New Orleans, and provided that all animals intended for consumption as food should be slaughtered there. It was the duty of the new corporation to permit any person to slaughter animals in its facilities at charges regulated by statute. The legislation purported to be a public health measure, and provided for the inspection of animals. Butchers of New Orleans attacked the statute as unconstitutional.

The Supreme Court, by 5–4 decision, upheld the statute.[6] The principal argument was over the meaning and application of the Privileges or Immunities Clause of the Fourteenth Amendment. The plaintiffs' contention was that before the adoption of the Constitution an individual, as citizen of his State, had certain fundamental rights to which he was entitled by reason of his State citizenship. By the Fourteenth Amendment, they argued, the citizen became primarily a citizen of the United States and only secondarily of the State; therefore, the fundamental rights which formerly attached to him as a citizen of the State now belonged to him as a citizen of the United States and cannot be abridged by the State; and one of his fundamental rights is to engage in a common calling or pursuit, such as the slaughtering of animals for food.

In an opinion by Justice Samuel F. Miller, the majority refused to accept this position. They held that the Privileges or Immunities Clause of the Fourteenth Amendment safeguards only the rights of citizens of the United States but not the rights of citizens of the States. There was no intention, said Justice Miller, to transfer from the States to the Federal government the security and protection of civil rights. To hold otherwise, he said,

would constitute this court a perpetual censor upon all legislation of the states, on the civil rights of their own citizens, with authority to nullify such as it did not approve. . . .

We are convinced that no such results were intended by the Congress which proposed these amendments, nor by the legislatures of the states which ratified them.

The only privileges and immunities within the ambit of the amendment, said the Court, were those "which owe their existence to the federal government, its national character, its Constitution, or its laws." Justice Miller enumerated the following rights as privileges and immunities that inhere in persons by virtue of their being citizens of the United States (as distinguished from their being citizens of their respective States):

against ex post facto laws (Article I, Section 10 of Constitution);
against bills of attainder (ibid.);
against laws impairing obligation of contracts (ibid.);
to come to the seat of his government to transact official business;
to enjoy free access to seaports;
to enjoy free access to subtreasuries and (Federal) land offices;
to enjoy free access to (Federal) courts of justice;
of assembly and to petition (Congress) for redress of grievances;
to writ of habeas corpus (Article I, Section 9);
to use navigable waters;
to privileges and immunities secured by treaties;
to privileges and immunities secured by the Civil War Amendments.

The Court conceived of these rights as ones which must flow out of national citizenship in a federal system, as, e.g., the right to travel to Washington, D. C., to transact some official matter; or which are expressly provided for in the Constitution as limitations on the power of States (Article I, Section 10); or rights provided for in treaties. In *Slaughter-House* the Court took the position that an American citizen must look primarily to his State for the enumeration and protection of his civil rights, and that, regardless of what Bingham or Howard may have said about the intent of Congress, the Privileges or Immunities Clause of the Fourteenth Amendment effected no radical change in the location of the power over civil rights; the clause did not vest American citizens with the rights which belong "to the citizens of all free governments."

It has been correctly noted that the privileges and immunities which *Slaughter-House* recognized as being protected by the clause had, in fact, been available to citizens even prior to 1868, so that the clause was, by the decision, reduced to a superfluous repetition, with the result that the clause enjoys the distinction—unique among constitutional provisions—of having been rendered a "practical nullity" by a single decision of the Supreme Court[7]

While *Slaughter-House* drew the teeth out of the clause, the provision has been allowed to play a minor role. The Court has recognized the right to pass freely from State to State as a right of national citizenship; also the right to vote for national officers, the right to enter public lands, the right to be protected against violence while in lawful Federal custody, the right to inform Federal authorities of violation of Federal laws, the right to acquire and retain property, the right to carry on interstate commerce, and the right to petition Congress for redress of grievances.[8]

III.

Except for few privileges and immunities, the majority in *Slaughter-House* held that, for the protection of his civil rights, the citizen must look to his State, for civil rights "are left to the State governments for security and protection, and not by this article [the Fourteenth Amendment] placed under the special care of the Federal government. . . . "

Although the Court's decision emasculated the Privileges or Immunities Clause, the dissenting opinions kept alive the spirit of Justice Washington's opinion in *Corfield*, and in later years contributed to the establishment and development of the idea of fundamental rights. From the perspective of history the dissenting opinions overshadow in significance the majority opinion and the Court's decision. Whatever living substance there is today in *Slaughter-House*, it is to be found mainly in the dissenting opinions.

In his dissenting opinion—in which he was joined by Chief Justice Salmon P. Chase and Justices Noah H. Swayne and Joseph P. Bradley—Justice Stephen J. Field moved the center of a person's citizenship from the State to the United States. By the Fourteenth Amendment, he said, the "fundamental rights, privileges and immunities which belong to him as a free man and a free citizen now belong to him as a citizen of the United States, and are not dependent upon his citizenship of any State." The Amendment assumes that there are privileges and immunities "which belong of right to citizens as such, and ordains that they shall not be abridged by state legislation." The Amendment, he said, "refers to the natural and inalienable rights which belong to all citizens"; they are those "which of right belong to the citizens of all free governments." The Amendment, Justice Field said, "was intended to give practical effect to the Declaration [of Independence] of 1776 of inalienable rights, rights which are the gift of the Creator; which the law does not confer, but only recognizes."

While Justice Bradley, as we have noted, concurred in the opinion of Justice Field, he wrote a separate dissenting opinion, in which he expressly referred to "fundamental rights" more than a half-dozen times. Although a State has broad and extensive powers to regulate the conduct of its citizens, "there are certain fundamental rights which this right of regulation cannot infringe." "I speak now," he said, "of the rights of citizens of any free government." Like Justice Field, Justice Bradley referred to the Declaration of Independence for the proposition that all men are "endowed by their Creator with certain inalienable rights; that among these are life, liberty and the pursuit of happiness," and went on to say:

> Here again we have the great three-fold division of the rights of man. Rights to life, liberty and the pursuit of happiness are equivalent to the rights of life, liberty and property. These are the fundamental rights . . . and these rights, I contend, belong to the citizens of every free government.

Justice Bradley spoke of the important rights guaranteed by the original Constitution and by the first set of amendments, and said that these rights are "among the privileges and immunities of citizens of the United States, or, what is still stronger for the force of the argument, the rights of all persons whether citizens or not." And then Justice Bradley went even beyond the express terms of the written Constitution. "But even if the Constitution were silent," he said, "the fundamental privileges and immunities of citizens, as such, would be no less real and no less inviolable than they now are. It was not necessary to say in words that the citizens of the United States should have and exercise all the privileges of citizens. . . . Their very citizenship conferred these privileges, if they did not possess them before." The purpose of the Fourteenth Amendment was simply to "provide national security against violation by the States of the fundamental rights of the citizen."

Justice Noah H. Swayne, while joining in the opinions of Justices Field and Bradley, wrote his own brief opinion, in which he, too, stressed the proposition that the Privileges or Immunities Clause of the Fourteenth Amendment guarantees to the American citizen "among other things, the fundamental rights of life, liberty and property, and also the rights which pertain to him by reason of his membership in the Nation." The citizen of a State, he said, does not have fewer fundamental rights; on the contrary, he has "the same fundamental rights as a citizen of the United States, and also certain others, local in their character, arising from his relation to the State. . . . "

While Justice Swayne only cited *Corfield*, Justices Field and Bradley each quoted from Justice Washington's opinion the passage concerning "those privileges and immunities which were, in their nature, fundamental; which belong of right to citizens of all free governments. . . . "

Before we leave these dissenting opinions it may be instructive, in the light of constitutional developments several generations later, to enumerate the privileges and immunities which Justice Bradley considered fundamental to American citizenship, or even as human rights to be enjoyed by every person under any free government. They are as follows:

protection by the government;
enjoyment of life and liberty;
right to acquire and possess property;
right to pursue and obtain happiness and safety;
right to pass through or reside in any other State;
benefit of writ of habeas corpus;
right to sue in state courts;
right to take, hold and dispose of property;
exemption from higher taxes than those paid by other citizens of the State;
to be free from bills of attainder;
to be free from ex post facto laws;
to be free from laws impairing obligation of contracts;
right of trial by jury;
right of free exercise of religious worship;
right of free speech and free press;
right peaceably to assemble for discussion of public measures;
right to be secure against unreasonable searches and seizures;
"and above all, and including all the rest, the right of not being deprived of life, liberty or property, without due process of law."

These, said Justice Bradley, would exist even if not named (as most of them are) in the Constitution. He took a broad view of the purposes of the Fourteenth Amendment:

The mischief to be remedied was not merely slavery and its incidents and consequences; but the spirit of insubordination and disloyalty to the national government which had troubled the country for so many years in some of the states, and that intolerance of free speech and free discussion which often rendered life and property insecure, and led to much unequal legislation. The amendment was an attempt to give voice to the strong national yearning ... in which American citizenship should be a sure guaranty of safety, and in which every citizen of the United States might stand erect in every portion of its soil, in *the full enjoyment of every right and privilege belonging to a freeman*, without fear of violence or molestation.[9]

IV.

In 1883, ten years after *Slaughter-House*, the Supreme Court had before it the question of the constitutionality of the Civil Rights Act of 1875, which provided that all persons shall be entitled to full and equal enjoyment of all accommodations and privileges of inns, public conveyances, theaters, and other places of public amusement. Violation of the act was made a criminal offense. The *Civil Rights Cases*[10] considered seven consolidated cases involving actions for denying to blacks accommodations of an inn or a hotel, a theater, the New York Grand Opera House, and of a ladies' car in a railway train. The Court, by 8–1 vote, held the act of Congress unconstitutional.

Justice Bradley, who as we have seen, wrote a strong dissenting opinion in *Slaughter-House*, wrote the opinion for the Court. Considering the case under the Fourteenth Amendment, the Court said that the amendment, by its express terms, is directed only at State action: "*No State*," it provides, "shall make or enforce" any law which shall abridge privileges or immunities of citizens of the United States; "nor shall *any State*" deprive a person of his life, liberty or property without due process of law, or deny to any person equal protection of the laws. But in the Civil Rights Act of 1875 Congress had attempted to regulate, not State, but *private* action. It is true that Section 5 of the amendment gives Congress the power to enact enforcement legislation, but this only means, said Justice Bradley, that Congress has the power to pass acts which will enforce the provisions of the Fourteenth Amendment, and this means the enactment of appropriate legislation directed at *State action*. The wrongful act of a private individual, "not sanctioned in some way by the State," "may presumably be vindicated by resort to the laws of the State for redress," but not by resort to a law enacted by Congress.

The Court then considered the Civil Rights Act under the Thirteenth Amendment, which provides that neither slavery nor involuntary servitude shall exist within the United States, and the amendment gives Congress power to enforce its provision by appropriate legislation. Now, this amendment speaks not only to the States but is "an absolute declaration that slavery or involuntary servitude shall not exist in any part of the United States." Congress, therefore, does have power to enact laws directed at private as well as State action that attempts to impose badges and incidents of slavery.

But what is slavery? What is "its substance and visible form"? The Court pointed to the following characteristics as defining slavery: compulsory labor for the master; restraint of the slave's movements except by the master's will; his inability to hold property, to make contracts, or to have standing in court, or to be a witness against a white person; severer punishment; "and such like burdens and incapacities." Such were "the inseparable incidents of the institution."

Opposed to the incidents of slavery are "those fundamental rights which are the essence of civil freedom," the rights which Congress set forth in the Civil Rights Act of 1866, the year following the ratification of the Thirteenth Amendment, and these are the right to make and enforce contracts, to sue, be parties, give evidence, and to inherit, purchase, lease, and sell property. These are "fundamental rights which appertain to the essence of citizenship, and the enjoyment or deprivation of which constitutes the essential distinction between freedom and slavery."

These rights, the Court held, do not include "what may be called the social rights of men and races in the community." When the owner of an inn, a public conveyance or a theater denies accommodations to an individual, "even though the denial be founded on the race or color of that individual," he is denying him a "social" right, which does not pertain to the essence of citizenship or freedom. "Where does any slavery or servitude, or badge of either," Justice Bradley asked rhetorically, "arise from such an act of denial? . . . What has it to do with the question of slavery?"

> Can the act of a mere individual, the owner of the inn, the public conveyance or place of amusement, refusing the accommodation, be justly regarded as imposing any badge of slavery or servitude . . . ? It would be running the slavery argument into the ground, to make it apply to every act of discrimination which a person may see fit to make as to the guests he will entertain, or as to the people he will take into his coach or cab or car, or admit to his concert or theater, or deal with in other matters of intercourse or business.

As we see, Justice Bradley carried over into the *Civil Rights Cases* his concern with the idea of fundamental rights which he had developed in his dissenting opinion in *Slaughter-House*. In the earlier case he was concerned with the right of a citizen "of any free government" to engage in a common calling. In the later case he was concerned with defining, in terms of fundamental rights, the essential distinction between slavery and freedom. In essence the Court's holding was that the Thirteenth Amendment was not to be read as a broad Declaration of the Rights of Man and of the Citizen, but only as an Emancipation Proclamation written into the Constitution. Its only purpose was to insure abolition constitutionally. Congress has "power to enforce this article by appropriate legislation"—this article, the Thirteenth Amendment, as it is written, and not an article that is not in the Constitution. And what is abolition? It means only, said Justice Bradley for the Court, free in the place of forced labor, contract and property rights, and, what is an indispensable condition for the enforcement and enjoyment of these rights, the status of a free man in the courts.

In an elaborate and eloquent dissenting opinion, Justice Harlan protested that this interpretation truncated the Thirteenth Amendment. The amendment, he said, guaranteed a state of freedom and gave Congress power to protect that freedom and the rights necessarily inhering in it. That freedom involved more than exemption from actual slavery. "Was it," Justice Harlan asked,

> the purpose of the Nation simply to destroy the institution [of slavery], and then remit the race . . . to the several States for such protection, in their civil rights, necessarily growing out of freedom, as those States, in their discretion, might choose to provide? Were the States against whose protest the institution was destroyed, to be left free . . . to make or allow discriminations against that race, as such, in the enjoyment of those fundamental rights which by universal concession, inhere in a state of freedom?

The intent of the amendment was not simply to eradicate the institution of slavery, but to eradicate also its badges and incidents; and to achieve these ends the amendment vested power in Congress to enact appropriate legislation, laws that would end the "burdens and disabilities, the necessary incidents of slavery, which constitute its substance and visible form," and to extend to members of the black race "such civil rights as belong to freemen of other races."

In his thinking, the first section of the Fourteenth Amendment meshed with the Thirteenth Amendment. The first clause of the first section provides that all persons born or naturalized in the United States are citizens of the United States and of the State wherein they reside. This provision has nothing to do with the problem of State action. As an affirmative grant from the Nation, citizenship may be protected by acts of Congress without regard to State laws or State action. As citizens, blacks are entitled to all privileges and immunities under Article IV, Section 2. What are those privileges and immunities? Justice Harlan answered this central question in the words of Justice Washington. They are "those which are fundamental in citizenship in a free republican government." By the Fourteenth Amendment, Negroes were made not only American citizens but also citizens of the States wherein they reside. Well, then, asked Justice Harlan,

> With what rights, privileges or immunities did this grant invest them? There is one, if there be no other: exemption from race discrimination in respect of any civil right belonging to citizens of the white race in the same State. . . . Citizenship in this country necessarily imports at least equality of civil rights among citizens of every race in the same State. It is fundamental in American citizenship that, in respect of such rights, there shall be no discrimination by the State or its officers, or by individuals or corporations exercising public functions or authority, against any citizen because of his race or previous condition of servitude.

With respect to the use of public conveyances, Justice Harlan argued that common carriers exercise a sort of public office, that railways are public highways, established by public authority for public use and benefit and subject to public control.

> Such being the relations these corporations held to the public, it would seem that the right of a colored person to use [a public conveyance], upon the terms accorded to freemen of other races, is as fundamental . . . as are any of the rights which my brethren concede to be so far fundamental as to be deemed the essence of civil freedom.

The same observations made as to public conveyances, said Justice Harlan, apply to inns and places of public amusement, all of which are established and maintained under licenses, and all of which are charged with duties to the general public in their exercise of public or quasi-public functions. Racial discrimination by such an agency imposes upon the Negro "a badge of servitude," which Congress may prohibit under the Thirteenth Amendment. Under the Fourteenth Amendment, a denial, by such agencies, of equality of civil rights is State action. "If it be not, then the race is left, in respect of the civil rights in question, practically at the mercy of corporations and individuals wielding power under the States."

Congress, said Justice Harlan, in enacting the Civil Rights Act of 1875 was not concerned with mere social rights, with which, of course, the government has nothing to do. "The right, for instance, of a colored citizen to use the accommodations of a public highway, upon the same terms as are permitted to white citizens, is no more a social right than his right, under the law, to use the public streets of a city or a town, or a turnpike road, or a public market, or a post-office, or his right to sit in a public building with others, of whatever race, for the purpose of hearing the political questions of the day discussed."

V.

What we have seen is an effort, a struggle, to legitimate, within the confines of the Constitution, the concept of fundamental rights. The first effort, initiated by Justice Washington, was to place fundamental rights under the protection of the Privileges or Immunities Clause of Article IV, Section 2. This approach has still some viability, as we will see in chapter 8.

The second attempt, initiated in dissenting opinions in *Slaughter-House*, was to have the Privileges or Immunities Clause of the Fourteenth Amendment embrace a guarantee of fundamental rights. The strong opinions of Justices Field, Bradley, and Swayne had, however, failed to persuade a majority of the Court, until 1999, as we will see.

The third try was made by the dissenting opinion of Justice Harlan in the *Civil Rights Cases*, in which he attempted to import into the words "privileges or immunities" as written in the Fourteenth Amendment, and as implied in the Thirteenth Amendment, the idea of civil rights, and then to make civil rights into fundamental rights—or fundamental rights into civil rights. Had Justice Harlan succeeded to persuade four other Justices of the Court in 1883, the history of the last hundred years of the United States would have been radically different.[11]

After *Slaughter-House*, for sixty-two years the Privileges or Immunities Clause of the Fourteenth Amendment was totally ignored by the Supreme Court. Then, in 1935, it was brought to life by a majority of the Court in *Colgate* v. *Harvey*,[12] which held invalid a Vermont income tax statute which discriminated against income from mortgages and notes based on loans made in other States. The Court held that it was a privilege or immunity of national citizenship to make loans in any part of the country. Justice Stone dissented in an opinion, joined by Justices Brandeis and Cardozo, in which he stated that the Privileges or Immunities Clause "had consistently been construed as protecting only interests, growing out of the relationship between the citizen and the national government, created by the Constitution and federal laws," and that since the adoption of the Fourteenth Amendment at least forty-four cases had been brought before the Court in which State statutes had been attacked under the Privileges or Immunities Clause and that in none of these cases had State legislation been held invalid under this clause. Five years later *Colgate* v. *Harvey* was overruled.[13]

In *Hague* v. *C.I.O.*[14] plaintiffs asserted that public officials of Jersey City were interfering with their right to hold public meetings in the city to discuss rights afforded by the National Labor Relations Act. Justice Owen J. Roberts, joined only by Justice Black, asserted that the right peaceably to assemble to discuss matters relating to a Federal act was a privilege inherent in national citizenship, and cited *Slaughter-House* in support.

In *Edwards* v. *California*[15] as many as four Justices raised their voices in support of a national privilege or immunity. The case involved a California statute aimed to prevent nonresident indigent persons from entering the State. The majority of the Court held the statute invalid under the Commerce Clause. Justice Douglas, joined by Justice Black and Justice Frank Murphy, concurred on the ground that the right of persons to move freely from State to State occupied a more protected position under the Constitution than does the movement of cattle, and that this right

is an incident of *national* citizenship protected by the privileges and immunities clause of the Fourteenth Amendment against state interference. . . .

This right, he said, was "a right fundamental to the national character of our Federal government." It is a right of "*national* citizenship."[16] It should be noted that Justice Douglas did not assert that the right to travel is a fundamental right, but that it is "a right fundamental to the national character of our Federal government," and *as such* was protected by the Privileges or Immunities Clause of the Fourteenth Amendment; and for this proposition he cited *Slaughter-House*.

Justice Robert H. Jackson concurred separately on the same ground. The Privileges or Immunities Clause was written into the Fourteenth

Amendment to make *national* citizenship the dominant and paramount allegiance among Americans. The return for this allegiance was protection, and this was the intent of the Citizenship and the Privileges or Immunities clauses of the Fourteenth Amendment.

> But the hope proclaimed in such generality soon shriveled in the process of judicial interpretation. For nearly three-quarters of a century this Court rejected every plea to the privileges and immunities clause. . . .
>
> While instances of valid "privileges or immunities" must be but few, I am convinced that this is one. . . . This Court has not been timorous about giving concrete meaning to such obscure and vagrant phrases as "due process," "general welfare," "equal protection," or even "commerce among the several States." But it has always hesitated to give any real meaning to the privileges and immunities clause lest it improvidently give too much.
>
> This Court should, however, hold squarely that it is a privilege of citizenship of the United States . . . to enter any state of the Union. . . . If national citizenship means less than this, it means nothing. . . .

As these concurring opinions by Justices Douglas and Jackson make clear, they, joined by Justices Black and Murphy, conceived of the right to travel from one State into another as a right fundamental to national citizenship, anchored in the Privileges or Immunities Clause of the Fourteenth Amendment. It was not until almost three decades later, in 1969, in *Shapiro* v. *Thompson*,[17] that a majority of the Court spoke of "the fundamental right of interstate movement" and declared that

> We have no occasion to ascribe the source of this right to travel interstate to a particular constitutional provision.

And the Court cited at this point *Corfield* and other cases which were based on the Comity Clause of Article IV, Section 2; *Slaughter-House* and other cases that involved the Privileges or Immunities Clause of the Fourteenth Amendment; and *Edwards*, which used the Commerce Clause.

We shall need to return to *Shapiro* v. *Thompson*, but at this point it is sufficient for us to note that, as recently as 1969, the Court by-passed a superb opportunity to follow the lead of Justices Douglas and Jackson and instill life into the Privileges or Immunities Clause by placing at least the fundamental right to travel under its guarantee. We were compelled to look elsewhere for the home and guarantee of rights in general and of fundamental rights in particular.

"As a matter of history," the late Professor Edward S. Corwin wrote,

> there can be little question that it was the intention of the Framers of the [Privileges or Immunities] clause [of the Fourteenth Amendment] to transmute all the ordinary rights of citizenship in a free government into rights of national citizenship, and thereby in effect to transfer their regulation and protection to the National Government.[18]

But unfortunately for the history of civil liberties and civil rights, the Supreme Court—except for some dissenting voices—had seen fit virtually to repeal the Privileges or Immunities Clause, and to relegate their protection to the States. In more recent years, as we shall see, the Court felt compelled to reclaim for the National Government the constitutional power and duty to define and protect fundamental rights, but this end it accomplished by following other constitutional routes and after the loss of precious years and the denial of life and liberty to countless Americans who had looked to their State in vain. In subsequent and more recent years, as will be seen, although the decisions practically nullifying the Privileges or Immunities Clause were not reversed, the minority Justices in the end have been vindicated: the fundamental rights *are* protected by the National Government. The spirit, if not the letter, of Justice Field's dissenting opinion in *Slaughter-House* has become the established constitutional law:

> The privileges and immunities . . . are those which of right belong to the citizens of all free governments. . . . [The Fourteenth Amendment] was intended to give practical effect to the Declaration [of Independence] of 1776 of inalienable rights, rights which are the gift of the Creator; which the law does not confer, but only recognizes.[19]

It has recently been argued that "the legal environment is now ripe for a privileges or immunities jurisprudence tied to conceptions of fundamental rights."[20] The argument is that since only the Privileges or Immunities Clause "seems to connote substantive content," a "fundamental rights approach seems natural for the language" of the clause.[21] This approach, it is contended, is preferable to the route chosen by the Supreme Court through the Equal Protection Clause; for the Court would then avoid the complex problem of evaluating legislative classifications. "The judicial command would be a clear statement that given our Constitution, our federated system, and our society's values, the right asserted . . . is so fundamental that the legislature may not infringe it in this fashion. This would seem to put the courts in an institutionally more tenable position." In this approach there would be no need for the Court to concern itself with the legislative purpose of the classification. Furthermore, it is said,

> much of the Supreme Court's strength and the degree of respect that it commands are directly tied to society's reverence for its written Constitution. Judicial review is on a firmer foundation when the Court acts directly to give meaning and content to the specific words of the Constitution, than when it acts through a methodological smokescreen. The doctrinal trappings of equal protection adjudication are ill-suited for widespread understanding and acceptance by the nation as a whole. Privileges or immunities interpretation would be far more straightforward. . . . [22]

These would be persuasive arguments if the adjudicatory slate were clean; if we were back in 1875 or even at the turn of the century. But to turn back the clock, to rewrite constitutional history may hardly advance public understanding and acceptance of constitutional doctrine. As we shall see, what Justices Washington, Field, Bradley and Harlan, and other Justices of the Court, sought to achieve through the concept of fundamental rights has, in fact, been won. The end has been reached by resort to other provisions of the Constitution. However, had these Justices been listened to, the end would have been reached sooner and with less fumbling and stumbling. But there are perils in making fresh starts, and the end result may not be enhanced.

VI.

When read from the perspective of the general sweep of constitutional interpretation, *Slaughter-House* stands for the proposition that the Fourteenth Amendment was not intended to displace the States as the guarantor of the civil rights of their citizens. When, however, one concentrates on the specific facts in the case, the magisterial decision by five Justices is that the opportunity to engage in one of the common callings in order to make a living is not a privilege or an immunity protected against State infringement by the Federal Constitution. The dissenting opinion of Justice Field brought out this aspect of the case in stark terms. The opportunity to make a living is, he argued, a natural right that a person has, that a person must have, an "inalienable right" that is God-given, that is not dependent on any act of grace by government. When Adam and Eve were expelled from the Garden of Eden, Adam was sent forth "to till the ground from which he was taken," for only by the sweat of his face would he be able to eat bread. The right to work was therefore a right that was "inalienable," a right that was as much a part of the man as his skin. It was therefore a "natural right," or what might later be called a fundamental right.[23]

Justice Field cited the English *Case on Monopolies*, decided in the English courts in the time of Queen Elizabeth I. The government had granted plaintiff the exclusive right to engage in the trade of playing-cards. In a case against the defendant, who was alleged to have infringed on the plaintiff's exclusive privilege, the court held that the granting of the monopoly violated a principle of the common law:

> All trades as well as mechanical as others, which prevent idleness . . . and exercise men and youth in labor for the maintenance of themselves and their families, and for the increase of their substance, . . . are profitable for the commonwealth, and therefore the grant to the plaintiff to have the sole making of them is against the common law and the benefit and liberty of the subject.[24]

The majority opinion in *Slaughter-House* did not say that a citizen does not have the civil right to work in a common calling; but if he has this right, he has it as a citizen of his State but not as a citizen of the United States. Such right may, indeed, be a fundamental right, but only the State and not the Federal Government will protect him in the enjoyment of this right. And what if the State deprives him of this right, as was done by the State granting the monopoly to a corporation? The butchers brought their actions in State courts, but these courts upheld such statutes as a legitimate exercise of the State's police power. The only recourse was to seek relief under the United States Constitution, but that door remained closed and locked for yet many years.

In *Slaughter-House* the Supreme Court in effect said that the people of the United States must look to their respective States for vindication of what they may claim to be their civil rights, no matter how "fundamental" those rights may be; and the *Civil Rights Cases* in effect said to the African-Americans that they cannot look to the Civil War Amendments for protection of, what the Court called, their "social rights," the right of equal enjoyment of places of public accommodation. It was only years later, when the Supreme Court began to take seriously *Corfield* and the dissenting opinions in *Slaughter-House* and in the *Civil Rights Cases*, and the principle of fundamental rights, that the Bill of Rights came to life, came to be meaningful and not mere rhetoric. But to see how this development came about, we shall still need to consider the dissenting opinions of Justices Field and Harlan, though written in cases other than the aforementioned ones.

VII.

To better understand the jurisprudential philosophy that underlies the great dissenting opinions of Justices Field and Harlan, it is necessary to consider, however briefly, the philosophy of Natural Law and Natural Rights on which their thought was built.

When Thomas Jefferson wrote in the Declaration of Independence that "all men are created equal," that all men enjoy "inalienable rights," that the inalienable rights of men include the right to "life, liberty and the pursuit of happiness," and that government exists to protect these rights, he did not think that he was stating anything that was novel. He knew that these propositions derived from the political writings of John Locke, which themselves flowed out of a long tradition known as Natural Law, that was found in Thomas Aquinas's *Summa Theologiae*, and in the teachings of the Stoics. Jefferson had no need to cite his sources or authorities, he rightly assumed that they were well known to the members of the committee to whom he submitted his draft, that included Benjamin Franklin, John Adams, Roger Sherman, and Robert Livingston. The Natural Law philosophy assumed that God, or the gods, provided an order for men just as was ordered for the material world—a moral order, a rational order, an eternal law that the mind of man can grasp. Natural Law assumes that men had certain duties toward one another, as social beings, and had certain rights that men must respect. These duties and rights existed before men instituted governments; governments are formed to enforce the duties and to protect the rights. According to John Locke, the basic duty of government is the protection of life, liberty, and property.[25]

Since the fundamental rights of men are given by Nature or by God, and inhere in men prior to government, one need not look for their protection to any statute or constitution. But a constitution can be helpful. For this reason Jefferson urged James Madison to frame and propose amendments to the Constitution that would spell out some of the fundamental rights, with, however, the understanding that there may be other fundamental rights, too, equally deserving of protection.[26]

Now, when Stephen Johnson Field took his seat on the Supreme

Court in 1863, and when John Marshall Harlan took his place on the Court in 1877, each brought with him, as an essential part of his intellectual and jurisprudential baggage, a firm belief in this philosophy, that they read into or attributed to the Constitution, especially the Privileges or Immunities Clause. But, be it noted, they believed, as did their predecessor Justice Washington, that it was not necessary to point to the Constitution for every conceivable inalienable right. In this they reflected the position taken by James Madison that, while it is all right to have a Bill of Rights, its provisions were not really indispensable, for a free government has only the rights and powers properly given to it by the people, and the inalienable rights of men are not given up—they cannot ever be given up—when a government is instituted. The fundamental rights are reserved by and to the people.

Many, perhaps most, Justices of the Supreme Court[27] shared a belief in the philosophy of Natural Law, but Justice Field—and to some extent also Justice Harlan—was most prominently identified with it. As the years moved on, and case after case was argued and decided, it became apparent that a major emphasis had been placed by the Court on the right to property as the most important inalienable, imprescritable natural right, the key to the right to the pursuit of happiness, that the government must respect and protect. Property became, in constitutional terms, the basic privilege or immunity. In terms of the Due Process Clause of the Fourteenth Amendment, the protection of the right of property became its most important objective.

It is necessary to note here that the Due Process Clause was understood to guaranty not only proper procedure—procedural due process—but also substantive rights, what came to be known as substantive due process, where the stress was placed on the words "liberty" or "property" rather than on procedure, so that, e. g., even if a statute provided the most detailed and correct procedure for the infringement of a property right, this did not necessarily save the statute if it deprived the owner of some substantial aspect of his property. It was this use—or misuse—of the philosophy of Natural Law that brought it into disrepute. It came to be identified as the *Lochner* theory of constitutional law which dominated the Court until the New Deal.

But the disparagement of the philosophy of Natural Law and Natural Rights, and the discrediting of *Lochner* jurisprudence, overlooked the fact that it was jurists like Justices Field, Harlan and Bradley who deserve credit for urging upon the Court the proposition that there are fundamental rights—besides the right to property!—that men must be said to have, and that no free government of free men has a lawful power to infringe or deny. When the Natural Law Justices are considered from this perspective, as they should be, then they are seen as the forerunners of Justices Holmes, Brandeis, Murphy, Rutledge, Warren, and Brennan. From the standpoint of law relating to economics, the Natural Law philosophy may be said to have been reactionary or overly conservative, but from the standpoint of civil liberties the same philosophy was liberal and libertarian.

It was Justices Field and Harlan and other Natural Law Justices who contended that certain rights are fundamental; that such rights are of universal applicability, that they are independent of government, that a person cannot rightly divest himself of these rights, that these rights are essential not only for the good life but for human life, that they are indispensable for human well-being.

It was the Natural Law Justices who introduced into American constitutional thought the belief that there is a hierarchy of rights, that some rights are fundamental, basic, undeniable, beyond the scope of argument or debate. What H. L. A. Hart wrote in 1955 was said long before him by dissenting Justices of the Supreme Court: There are certain rights, he said, that

> are not rights under the ordinary law but *fundamental rights* which may be said to be against the legislature, limiting its powers to make (or unmake) the ordinary law, where so to do would be to deny individuals certain freedoms and benefits now regarded as essentials of human well-being, such as freedom of speech and of association, freedom from arbitrary arrest, security of life and person, . . . [28]

This has a modern, even contemporary, ring, but to one with a historical sense it resonates with thoughts of Sophocles, of Cicero, and, yes, of Justice Field and of Justice Harlan.

Notes

1. *Corfield* v. *Coryell*, 6 Fed. Cas. 546 (1823).
2. *Dred Scott* v. *Sandford*, 60 U.S. (19 How.) 393 (1857).
3. Quoted in Jacobus tenBroek, *The Anti-Slavery Origins of the Fourteenth Amendment* (Berkeley, 1951), 211–212.
4. Ibid., pp. 212–213.
5. Ibid., pp. 220–221. See also Robert J. Harris, *The Quest for Equality* (Baton Rouge, 1960), 35–36; Alexander M. Bickel, "The Original Understanding and the Segregation Decision," 69 *Harv. L. Rev.* 1 (1955), reprinted in *Selected Essays on Constitutional Law* (ed. Ass'n. Am. Law Schools, 1963); Howard J. Graham,

"Our Declaratory Fourteenth Amendment," 7 *Stanford L. Rev.* 3 (1954). Cf. Jos. B. James, *The Framing of the Fourteenth Amendment* (Urbana, 1956).

6. *Slaughter-House Cases*, 16 Wall. (83 U.S.) 36 (1873).

7. *The Constitution of the United States of America*, Congressional Research Service. Library of Congress, (Washington, D.C. 1987), 1471 ff.

8. Ibid., pp. 1471–1472. Cf. Tribe, L. H. *American Constitutional Law* (Mineola, N.Y., 2nd ed., 1988), 528 ff.

9. Italics supplied.

10. *Civil Rights Cases*, 109 U.S. 3 (1883).

11. The public accommodations provisions of the Civil Rights Act of 1964 were based by Congress on the Equal Protection Clause and Section 5 of the Fourteenth Amendment and on the power of Congress to regulate interstate commerce under Article 1, Section 8 of the Constitution. See *Heart of Atlanta Motel* v. *United States*, 379 U. S. 241 (1964).

12. *Colgate* v. *Harvey*, 296 U.S. 404 (1935). The majority opinion was by Justice Sutherland.

13. *Madden* v. *Kentucky*, 309 U.S. 83 (1940).

14. *Hague* v. *C.I.O.*, 307 U.S. 496 (1939).

15. *Edwards* v. *California*, 314 U.S. 160 (1941)

16. Italics in original.

17. *Shapiro* v. *Thompson*, 394 U.S. 618 (1969).

18. Edw. S. Corwin, *The Constitution and What It Means Today* (Princeton, 1978 ed.) 461.

19. *Slaughter-House Cases*, 16 Wall (83 U.S.) 36 (1873).

20. Norman G. Benoit, "The Privileges or Immunities Clause of the Fourteenth Amendment: Can There Be Life After Death?" *Suffolk U. Law Rev.* 11:61, 101 (1976).

21. Ibid., at pp. 101, 104. See John Hart Ely, *Democracy and Distrust* (Cambridge, Mass., 1980).

22. Ibid., at p. 105.

23. The position taken by Benoit (see *supra* note 20) was first stated by Philip B. Kurland, "The Privileges or Immunities Clause: 'Its Hour Came Round at Last,' 9 *Wash. U. Law Quarterly* 405 (1972).

 The literature on the Privileges or Immunities Clause of the Fourteenth Amendment often expresses concern that its guarantee protects only citizens and does not, therefore, benefit aliens. Both Kurland and Benoit meet this point with the argument that where aliens are concerned, the Equal Protection Clause would afford them identical protection. See Kurland at p. 415, Benoit at p. 109.

 In this connection note may be taken of the fact that the use of the word "citizens" in the Comity Clause of Article IV, Section 2, has not been interpreted restrictively. The terms "citizen" and "resident" are "essentially interchangeable." See *Baldwin* v. *Montana Fish and Game Commission,* 436 U.S. 371 (1978), at 397, note 2, and *Hicklin* v. *Orbeck*, 437 U.S. 518 (1978), at 524, note 8. John Hart Ely, in his work cited in note 21 above, suggests that the Privileges or Immunities Clause of the Fourteenth Amendment should be read as intending to define a class of rights rather than as discriminating between two classes of person, citizens and non-citizens.

24. Cited by Justice Field at p. 103. See Hadley Arkes, *The Return of George Sutherland* (Princeton, 1994), 63.

25. John Locke, *Two Treaties of Government*, ed. P. Laslett (Cambridge University Press, 1960).

26. *Life and Selected Letters of Thomas Jefferson*, ed. A. Koch and W. Peden (New York, 1944), 436.
27. *American Interpretations of Natural Law*, Benj. F. Wright (Harvard University Press, 1931); Chas. G. Haines, *The Revival of Natural Law Concepts* (Harvard University Press, 1930).
28. H. L. A. Hart, "Are There Any Natural Rights?" *Philosophical Rev.*, 64 (1955): 175–91.

3

The Bill of Rights: A Bill of Fundamental Rights

I.

We have seen that, despite rebuffs, Justices of the Supreme Court, time and again in strong dissenting opinions, affirmed their belief that fundamental rights are privileges and immunities guaranteed by the Constitution against denial or abridgment by the States. What are these fundamental rights? Perhaps the fullest and broadest enumeration of such rights was formulated by Justice Bradley in *Slaughter-House*.[1] His dissenting opinion is historically notable, however, for another reason, for we find in it, for the first time, the contention that Section 1 of the Fourteenth Amendment somehow "incorporates" the first eight amendments of the Constitution, that the rights enumerated in the Bill of Rights are

> among the privileges and immunities of citizens of the United States, or what is still stronger for the force of the argument, the rights of all persons whether citizens or not.

Since Justice Bradley made this contention in 1873, it has had an erratic career in constitutional jurisprudence, and has been disputed and refined, but the essence of Justice Bradley's idea has won out and has become firmly fixed as constitutional doctrine. We can trace here only the main lines of this highly significant aspect of the idea of fundamental rights.

43

Three years later, in 1876, the Court decided, what was perhaps the first case in which the claim was explicitly made, that one of the provisions of the Bill of Rights formulated a privilege or an immunity which a State may not infringe. In *Walker* v. *Sauvinet*,[2] the defendant claimed that Louisiana had denied him a trial by jury in violation of the Seventh Amendment to the Constitution, which provides that "In suits at common law, where the value in controversy shall exceed $20, the right of trial by jury shall be preserved." The Supreme Court, by 7–2 vote, held that a trial by jury in suits at common law in State courts is not a privilege or immunity of national citizenship.

Justice Field and Justice Nathan Clifford dissented from the judgment and opinion, but it is noteworthy that Justice Bradley did not dissent. A possible inference from this fact may be that he had not meant, in his *Slaughter-House* opinion, that *all* of the amendments comprising the Bill of Rights were to be given equal dignity and that *all* were to be enforced against the States—a view which later came to be known as "selective incorporation."

In the same year the Court decided the famous case of *United States* v. *Cruikshank*,[3] in which defendants had been indicted under a Federal statute for having deprived certain citizens of their right peaceably to assemble "for a peaceful and lawful purpose." The Court held the indictment inadequate because it failed to allege *that the assembly was for a purpose related to the Federal Government*. Chief Justice Morrison R. Waite wrote:

> The right of the people peaceably to assemble for the purpose of petitioning for a redress of grievances, or for anything else connected with the powers or the duties of the national government, is an attribute of national citizenship, and, as such, under the protection of and guaranteed by, the United States. . . . If it had been alleged in these counts that the object of the defendants was to prevent a meeting for such a purpose, the case would have been within the statute, and within the scope of the sovereignty of the United States.

The reasoning here, as in *Slaughter-House*, was restrictive of the idea of fundamental rights, nationally guaranteed and nationally enforced. It concedes only that

> The very idea of a government, republican in form, implies a right on the part of its citizens to meet peaceably for consultation in respect to public affairs and to petition for redress of grievances.

This is the right of assembly as it was seen by Justice Miller in

Slaughter-House, viz., like the right of an American citizen to travel to Washington to transact some official matter.

In *Hurtado* v. *California*,[4] decided in 1884, the defendant had been found guilty of first-degree murder in a proceeding in the California courts that had been initiated by information rather than by grand jury indictment. Hurtado contended that execution of the judgment would mean the deprivation of his life or liberty without due process of law in violation of the Fourteenth Amendment. The Supreme Court upheld the judgment of conviction, stating that the process guarantees "not particular forms of procedure, but the very substance of individual rights to life, liberty, and property," and held that the substitution of a proceeding by information for indictment by a grand jury is not a denial of the "very substance" of an individual right. The Court took note of the wording of the Fifth Amendment: that it provided for proceeding by presentment or indictment by a grand jury in cases involving a capital or otherwise infamous crime, that it prohibited double jeopardy, that in criminal cases a person shall not be compelled to be a witness against himself, and that private property shall not be taken for public use without just compensation; and the amendment contains the general provision that a person shall not "be deprived of life, liberty, or property, without due process of law." The Court reasoned that the requirement of proceeding by indictment must have been excluded from the concept of due process, otherwise it would have made no sense to require it so explicitly.

Justice Harlan wrote a strongly-worded dissenting opinion, in which he contended that the Court's reasoning would lead to the absurd and malicious conclusion that double jeopardy, compulsory self-incrimination, and expropriation of private property without just compensation would also not violate the due process requirement.

But Justice Harlan went beyond questions of constitutional interpretation. He pointed out that the Court's reasoning

> indubitably leads to the conclusion that but for the specific provisions made in the Constitution for the security of the personal rights enumerated, the general inhibition against the deprivation of life, liberty, and property without due process of law would not have prevented Congress from enacting a statute in derogation of them.

Justice Harlan thus broached the idea of the Due Process Clause, whether in the Fifth or in the Fourteenth Amendment, being open-ended and receptive to ideals of human decency not specifically enumerated in the written Constitution. Furthermore, Justice Harlan contended for a single standard of due process whether one reads the guarantee of the Fifth Amendment against Federal abridgment or of the Fourteenth Amendment against State action. "'Due process of law,' within the meaning of the national Constitution," he wrote,

> does not import one thing with reference to the powers of the States, and another with reference to the powers of the general government. If particular proceedings conducted under the authority of the general government, and involving life, are prohibited, because not constituting due process of law required by the Fifth Amendment . . . , similar proceedings, conducted under the authority of a State, must be deemed illegal as not being due process of law within the meaning of the Fourteenth Amendment.

While Justice Harlan's opinion cannot be read as an explicit argument for "incorporation" of the Fifth Amendment into the Due Process Clause of the Fourteenth Amendment, his language strongly suggests "incorporation," and certainly proposes a single standard of fundamental rights, as encased in the guarantee of due process, as against both the Federal Government and the States equally.

As we have seen, *Walker* v. *Sauvinet* perhaps was, in 1876, the first case in which the explicit claim was made that a provision of the Bill of Rights—the Seventh Amendment, relating to trial by jury in civil suits—constituted a privilege or immunity which a State may not infringe. The second case to test the theory of "incorporation" was *Presser* v. *Illinois*,[5] decided ten years later. The defendant in this case argued that the guarantee of the Second Amendment—"the right of the people to keep and bear arms, shall not be infringed"—was a guarantee also against the States, under the Citizenship and the Privilege or Immunities clauses of the Fourteenth Amendment. The Court held that the Second Amendment has no other effect than to restrict the powers of the Federal Government, and has no relation to the powers of a State.

In the following year, 1887, a defendant who had been convicted of murder and sentenced by the courts of Illinois to be executed claimed that he had not been convicted by an impartial jury and had been subjected to self-incrimination, and had thus been denied privileges or immunities guaranteed to him by the United States Constitution. In *Ex parte Spies*[6] the Supreme Court held that the Fourth Amendment against unreasonable searches and seizures, the Fifth Amendment guarantee against compulsory self-incrimination, and the Sixth Amendment guarantee to a speedy trial by an impartial jury, had no application to a State. Writing for a unanimous Court, Chief Justice Waite said:

That the first ten articles of amendment [the Bill of Rights] were not intended to limit the powers of the state governments in respect to their own people, but to operate on the National Government alone, was decided more than a half century ago, and that decision has been steadily adhered to since. . . . [7]

It was contended, however, in argument, that "though originally the first ten amendments were adopted as limitations on federal power, yet in so far as they secure and recognize fundamental rights—common-law rights—of the man, they make them privileges and immunities of the man as a citizen of the United States, and cannot now be abridged by a State under the Fourteenth Amendment. In other words, while the ten amendments as limitations on power only apply to the Federal Government, and not to the States, yet in so far as they declare or recognize rights of persons, these rights are theirs, as citizens of the United States, and the Fourteenth Amendment as to such rights limits state power, as the ten amendments had limited federal power."

This was the first case in which a litigant contended that although admittedly the guarantees of the Bill of Rights were not, as such, limits on the States, yet in so far as the amendments declared what were fundamental rights of man, they were privileges or immunities of citizens of the United States and were, therefore, since adoption of the Fourteenth Amendment, protected against abridgment by the State.[8] The Court chose to by-pass this transcendently important question and to decide the case against the defendant on other grounds.

But from this time forth the issue of fundamental rights, protected by the Fourteenth Amendment against State action, will come up time and again. The argument for the defendant in *Spies* gathered up into itself suggestions, intimations, nuances, and gropings found earlier, as we have noted, in dissenting opinions of Justices Bradley and Harlan,[9] and in those of Justices Field and Swayne, and first of all in the opinion of Justice Washington in *Corfield*, covering a span of over six decades.

II.

The argument for fundamental rights made on behalf of the defendant in *Spies* was lost on the Supreme Court but not on counsel practicing before the Court, and it was not long before the Court felt that it had to face the issue squarely.

In 1890, three years after *Spies*, the Court had before it *Ex parte Kemmler*,[10] in which the defendant, convicted of murder in the first degree, had been sentenced to die in the electric chair, under a statute adopted by the New York Legislature two years before. The defendant contended that the new means of execution were a form of cruel and unusual punishment, so that the statute was unconstitutional. The contention was summarized by Chief Justice Melville W. Fuller in the following terms:

> It is not contended, as it could not be, that the Eighth Amendment [prohibiting the infliction of cruel and unusual punishments] was intended to apply to the States, but it is urged that the provision of the Fourteenth Amendment, which forbids a State to make or enforce any law which shall abridge the privileges or immunities of citizens of the United States, is a prohibition on the State from the imposition of cruel and unusual punishments, and that such punishments are also prohibited by inclusion in the term "due process of law."

Chief Justice Fuller, in an opinion for a unanimous Court, upheld the constitutionality of the New York statute and the decisions of the State courts against the claims of the defendant. The Court followed the reasoning of *Slaughter-House* and *Cruikshank,* and said:

> Protection to life, liberty and property rests, primarily, with the States, and the [Fourteenth] Amendment furnishes an additional guaranty against any encroachment by the States upon those fundamental rights which belong to citizenship. . . . The privileges and immunities of citizens of the United States, as distinguished from the privileges and immunities of citizens of the States, are indeed protected by it; but those are privileges and immunities arising out of the nature and essential character of the national government. . . .

So much for the Privileges or Immunities Clause; but what of the applicability of the Due Process Clause? The Court on this question followed the reasoning of *Hurtado.* The Fifth Amendment provides for due process, but it also expressly guarantees grand jury indictment, prohibits double jeopardy and compulsory self-incrimination. So that the due process provision should not appear to be superfluous, the Court in *Hurtado* held that due process does not embrace the other three express guarantees. Now Chief Justice Fuller seemed to argue that since the Eighth Amendment expressly prohibits cruel and unusual punishments, this guarantee must be excluded from the reach of the due process guarantee of the Fourteenth Amendment.

What, then, does the Due Process Clause of the Fourteenth Amendment mean? The words, said the Court,

> refer to that law of the land in each State, which derives its authority from the inherent and reserved powers of the State, exerted within the limits of those fundamental principles of liberty and justice which lie at the base of all our civil and

political institutions. Undoubtedly the Amendment forbids any arbitrary deprivation of life, liberty or property, and [by the Equal Protection Clause?] secures equal protection to all under like circumstances in the enjoyment of their rights; and, in the administration of criminal justice, requires that no different or higher punishment shall be imposed upon one than is imposed upon all for like offenses [again, under the Equal Protection Clause?].

In the following year, 1891, another defendant[11] sentenced to death under the same statute of the State of New York, contended that the provision in the statute requiring his solitary confinement for some weeks before the time of his execution constituted cruel and unusual punishment and brought the statute "within the inhibition of the 8th Amendment to the federal Constitution." Again the Court unanimously rejected the argument; but again, the case is significant because of the nature of the claim made for the defendant—as restated by Chief Justice Fuller,

> that so far as those [first ten] amendments secure the fundamental rights of the individual, they make them his privileges and immunities as a citizen of the United States, which cannot now, under the Fourteenth Amendment, be abridged by a State; that the prohibition of cruel and unusual punishments is one of these; and that that prohibition is also included in that "due process of law" without which no State can deprive any person of life, liberty, or property.

The Court held that the *Kemmler* case was decisive of this case, and took occasion once more to state that

> The first ten articles of amendment were not intended to limit the powers of the States in respect of their own people, but to operate on the federal government only.

This proposition did not really answer defendant's contention, which was not simply that the Fourteenth Amendment "incorporated" the Eighth Amendment, but rather that the Privileges or Immunities Clause and the Due Process Clause guaranteed individual fundamental rights against abridgment by the States.

It was in *O'Neil* v. *Vermont*,[12] decided in 1892, that two Justices, Field and Harlan, took occasion to formulate explicitly and definitively, what has come to be known as the "incorporation" doctrine. Like the several preceding cases, this case, too, involved the claim of cruel and unusual punishment. The defendant, a resident in the State of New York, received orders for small quantities of intoxicating liquors from persons residing in Vermont. He sent the liquors by express. These transactions had extended over a period of three years.

O'Neil was convicted by the Vermont courts of 307 offenses under the State's statute regulating the sale of intoxicating beverages and was fined twenty dollars and sentenced to a month's imprisonment for each offense; and for failing or refusing to pay the fines and costs, he was to be confined three days for each dollar, making a total of 19,914 days of imprisonment—a period of over fifty-four years.

While a majority of the Supreme Court held that the issue of cruel and unusual punishment had not been properly raised, they took occasion to say:

> The mere fact that cumulative punishments may be imposed for distinct offenses in the same prosecution is not material upon this question. If the penalty were unreasonably severe for a *single* offense, the constitutional question might be urged; but here the unreasonableness is only in the number of offenses which the respondent has committed. We forbear the consideration of this question, . . . Moreover, as a Federal question, it has always been ruled that the 8th Amendment to the Constitution of the United States does not apply to the states.

In a long dissenting opinion, Justice Field acknowledged that previous to the adoption of the Fourteenth Amendment, it had been settled[13] that the Bill of Rights was not applicable to the States. This would still be the case, he went on, but for the Privileges or Immunities Clause of the Fourteenth Amendment. What are these privileges or immunities? "It may be difficult," he said,

> to define the terms so as to cover all the privileges and immunities of citizens of the United States, but after much reflection I think the definition given at one time before this court by a distinguished advocate—Mr. John Randolph Tucker, of Virginia—is correct, that the privileges and immunities of citizens of the United States are such as have their recognition in or guaranty from the Constitution of the United States. This definition is supported by reference to the history of the first ten amendments to the Constitution, and of the amendments which followed the late Civil War. . . .

Then Justice Field tied together the Citizenship Clause and the Privileges or Immunities Clause of the Fourteenth Amendment: those who are, by constitutional provision, citizens of the United States are entitled to all the privileges and immunities of such citizens. While, therefore, the first ten amendments, as limitations on power, are applicable only to the Federal Government,

> yet, so far as they declare or recognize the rights of persons, they are rights belonging to them as citizens of the United States under the Constitution. And the 14th Amendment, as to all such rights, places a limit upon state power by ordain-

ing that no State shall make or enforce any law which shall abridge them. If I am right in this view, then every citizen of the United States is protected from punishments which are cruel and unusual. It is an immunity which belongs to him, against both state and Federal action. . . . These rights, as those of citizens of the United States, find their recognition and guaranty against Federal action in the Constitution of the United States, and against state action in the 14th Amendment.

Justice Harlan concurred in these views but added his own dissenting opinion, in which he said that

since the adoption of the 14th Amendment, no one of the fundamental rights of life, liberty, or property, recognized and guaranteed by the Constitution of the United States, can be denied or abridged by a State in respect to any person within its jurisdiction. These rights are, principally, enumerated in the earlier amendments of the Constitution. . . . The Constitution was ratified in the belief, and only because of the belief, encouraged by its leading advocates, that immediately upon the organization of the Government of the Union, articles of amendment would be submitted to the people, recognizing those essential rights of life, liberty, and property. . . . Among those rights is immunity from cruel and unusual punishments, secured by the 8th Amendment against Federal action, and by the 14th Amendment against denial or abridgment by the states.[14]

Justice Field seems to have urged simply the idea that the Fourteenth Amendment "incorporates" the guarantees of the first ten amendments as privileges and immunities of American citizens—a view, as we shall see, later urged by Justice Black. Justice Harlan, however, urged a broader principle; namely, that the Fourteenth Amendment guarantees "the *fundamental rights* of life, liberty, [and] property"; that these fundamental rights are only principally enumerated in the Bill of Rights. This position, as will be seen, was due to have much wider appeal and acceptance.

In a case decided in 1900 Justice Harlan reinforced his position in elaborate and vigorous terms. In *Maxwell* v. *Dow*[15] the defendant had not been indicted but was tried on information charging him with robbery, and was convicted by a jury composed of only eight jurors, under proceedings authorized by laws of the State of Utah. The defendant contended that the prosecution by information and the trial by a jury of only eight persons abridged his privileges and immunities under the Fifth, Sixth, and Fourteenth Amendments, and that his trial and subsequent imprisonment deprived him of his liberty without due process of law in violation of the Fourteenth Amendment. By a vote of 8–1 the Supreme Court rejected these claims and affirmed the judgment of conviction.

The contentions on behalf of the defendant were summarized in the Court's opinion as follows:

> It is claimed . . . that since the adoption of the Fourteenth Amendment the effect of [the first ten] amendments has been thereby changed and greatly enlarged. It is now urged in substance that all the provisions contained in the first ten amendments, so far as they secure and recognize the fundamental rights of the individual as against the exercise of Federal power, are by virtue of [the Fourteenth] amendment to be regarded as privileges or immunities of a citizen of the United States, and therefore the states cannot provide for any procedure in state courts which could not be followed in a Federal court because of the limitations contained in those [first ten] amendments.

The Court, reviewing and re-affirming its precedents, such as *Slaughter-House*, *Cruikshank*, and *Walker* v. *Sauvinet*, held that the asserted privileges and immunities did not arise out of the nature or essential character of the National Government, and therefore were rights which rested with the State governments and were not protected by the Fourteenth Amendment. "These are matters," said the Court, "which have no relation to the character of the Federal government."

In his dissenting opinion Justice Harlan asked

> What are the privileges and immunities of "citizens of the United States?" Without attempting to enumerate them, it ought to be deemed safe to say that such privileges and immunities embrace *at least* those expressly recognized by the Constitution of the United States and placed beyond the power of Congress to take away or impair.[16]

Prior to the adoption of the Fourteenth Amendment, it was one of the privileges or immunities of American citizens that they should not be tried for crime in any Federal court except by a jury composed of twelve persons.[17] How can it be, asked Justice Harlan,

> that a citizen of the United States may be now tried in a state court for crime, particularly for an infamous crime, by eight jurors, when [the Fourteenth] Amendment expressly declares that "no state shall make or enforce any law which shall abridge the privileges or immunities of citizens of the United States"? . . .
>
> I am also of the opinion that the trial of the accused for the crime charged against him by a jury of eight persons was not consistent with the "due process of law" prescribed by the Fourteenth Amendment.

With extraordinary prescience, Justice Harlan anticipated the consequences of the Court's decision—unless, as was to be the case, the Court would in the future adopt a different principle with respect to the guarantee of fundamental rights under the Fourteenth Amendment. To say to any people that they do not enjoy "the privileges and immunities specified in the first ten Amendments," wrote Justice Harlan, "is to say that they do not enjoy real freedom."

> But suppose a state should prohibit the free exercise of religion; or abridge the freedom of speech or of the press; or forbid its people from peaceably assembling to petition the government for a redress of grievances; or authorize soldiers in time of peace to be quartered in any house without the consent of the owner. . . . These or any of these things being done by a state, this court, according to the reasoning and legal effect of the opinion just delivered, would be bound to say that the privileges and immunities specified were not privileges and immunities of citizens of the United States within the meaning of the Fourteenth Amendment. . . . Suppose the state of Utah should amend its Constitution and make the Mormon religion the established religion of the state, to be supported by taxation on all the people of Utah. Could its right to do so . . . be gainsaid under the principles of the opinion just delivered? . . . The privileges and immunities specified in the first ten Amendments as belonging to the people of the United States are equally protected by the Constitution. No judicial tribunal has authority to say that some of them may be abridged by the states while others may not be abridged. . . . There is no middle position, unless it be assumed to be one of the functions of the judiciary by an interpretation of the Constitution to mitigate or defeat what its members may deem the erroneous or unwise action of the people in adopting the Fourteenth Amendment. . . . If some of the guaranties of life, liberty, and property which at the time of the adoption of the national Constitution were regarded as fundamental and as absolutely essential to the enjoyment of freedom, have in the judgment of some ceased to be of practical value, it is for the people of the United States so to declare by an amendment of that instrument.

The difference between Justices Field and Harlan, on the one hand, and the majority of the Court, on the other, may be said to have been that the latter failed and refused to look beyond the facts of the cases before the Court, while the former allowed themselves to project imaginatively situations in which it would be morally impossible for the Court to simply reiterate the doctrine that the Bill of Rights comprised guarantees that restrained only the Federal Government. Suppose a State provided for punishment by slow, protracted physical torture, or death by burning or dismembering[18]—would the Court have persisted in adhering to precedents that held that the guarantee against cruel and unusual punishments applied only against the Federal Government? Suppose a state enacted a statute the intent and effect of which was to ban all newspapers with a circulation of less than ten thousand copies—would the Court have held that the State was in no way bound by the guarantees of the First Amendment? The dissenters on the Court, particularly Justice Harlan, could imagine—and foresee—the challenge of such situations, and so were deeply concerned with the question of fundamental rights, and the way this question could implicate the application of the Bill of Rights to State action. There might be reasonable differences of opinion as to whether a defendant in a criminal case was entitled to trial by a jury of twelve instead of eight persons, but suppose the State denied the defendant a jury trial altogether?[19] The basic question, for the dissenters, was the question of constitutional principle; its application to particular sets of facts was of secondary importance; and they—particularly Justice Harlan—resolved the basic question by refusing to see only the case before them. They were mindful of the instruction given by Chief Justice John Marshall: "We must never forget that it is a constitution we are expounding."[20]

III.

Our interest in this discussion is centered, not on the philosophy or process of the "incorporation" of the first eight or ten amendments into the Fourteenth Amendment, but on the emergence and development of the idea of fundamental rights, as the idea made its way in American constitutional law. But as we have seen, the question of fundamental rights became intertwined with the question of "incorporation" soon after the adoption of the Fourteenth Amendment, and the two questions have continued to overlap, and are still not altogether divorced.

The importance of the contribution to these developments made by Justices Field and Harlan can hardly be exaggerated. Justice Field served on the Court to 1897, Justice Harlan to 1911. Thus, when *Maxwell* v. *Dow* was decided in 1900, Justice Field was not there to support Justice Harlan. In 1908 Justice Harlan had his last opportunity to argue for his position, and he was a lone dissenter.

This was in the important case of *Twining* v. *New Jersey*.[21] The defendants, convicted by New Jersey courts of a misdemeanor, claimed that they had been subjected to compulsory self-incrimination. On behalf of the defendants it was argued that where a *fundamental right* guaranteed by one of the first ten amendments is involved, as here, then the Supreme Court has jurisdiction because of the guarantee of the Fourteenth Amendment that no State shall abridge privileges or immunities, or deny due process of law; that the history of the adoption of this amendment shows that the privilege against self-incrimination was considered *a fundamental right*; that the laws of a State come under the prohibition of this amendment when they infringe *fundamental rights*; that there are certain immutable principles of justice which inhere in the very idea of free government which no State may disregard, and that these principles, recognizing the inherent rights of the individual, are intended to be protected by the Fourteenth Amendment; that since the adoption of this amendment, none of the *fundamental rights* may be denied or abridged by a State; and that these *fundamental rights* are principally enumerated in the first ten amendments.

It should be noted that the defendants did not claim the protection of the provision of the Fifth Amendment that "no person . . . shall be compelled in any criminal case to be a witness against himself," for they recognized that it had been settled that the first ten amendments were not operative against the States. Their argument, as restated by the Court, was that the privilege against self-incrimination was

> one of the fundamental rights of national citizenship, placed under national protection by the 14th Amendment, and it is specifically argued that the "privileges and immunities of citizens of the United States," protected against state action by that Amendment, include those fundamental rights which were protected against national action by the first eight Amendments; that this was the intention of the framers of the 14th Amendment, . . .

In other words, the basic claim was that the Fourteenth Amendment guaranteed *fundamental rights* against their abridgment by any State, and that the first eight amendments were evidence of what are some of the fundamental rights.

In his opinion for the Court, Justice William H. Moody, citing precedents and especially *Slaughter-House*, reiterated the proposition that a citizen's fundamental rights were protected (if at all) only by the States; that Justice Washington's enumeration of such rights in *Corfield* was to be treated "as rights of state citizenship under state protection." Furthermore, the Court held that the Fourteenth Amendment did not forbid the States to abridge the rights enumerated in the first eight amendments, because "those rights were not within the meaning of the clause 'privileges and immunities of citizens of the United States'." The Court also held that compulsory self-incrimination in a State trial was not a denial of due process.

In considering the due process claim, the Court made an important admission. It conceded that though some of the rights safeguarded by the Bill of Rights may not be privileges or immunities protected against abridgment by the States, a denial of them may nonetheless be a denial of due process. "If this is so," said Justice Moody, "it is not because those rights are enumerated in the first eight Amendments, but because they are of such a nature that they are included in the conception of due process."

The Court thus opened up the possibility of a constitutional link between fundamental rights and due process. This conclusion was reinforced by some propositions about the meaning of due process formulated by Justice Moody or quoted with approval by him from prior cases:

> [N]o change in ancient procedure can be made which disregards those fundamental principles, to be ascertained from time to time by judicial action, which have relation to process of law, and protect the citizen in his private right, and guard him against the arbitrary action of government. . . . It is sufficient to say [with regard to the meaning of due process of law] that there are certain immutable principles of justice which inhere in the very idea of free government which no member of the Union may disregard. The same words [due process] refer to that law of the land in each state, which derives its authority from the inherent and reserved powers of the state, exerted within the limits of those fundamental principles of liberty and justice which lie at the base of all our civil and political institutions. . . . such procedure [by the State in civil and criminal cases] must not work a denial of fundamental rights. . . . We have considered whether the right is so fundamental in due process that a refusal of the right is a denial of due process.

The Court held that it would be straining the meaning of due process to include within it a guarantee against compulsory self-incrimination. But as it reached this conclusion at the end of a long opinion, the Court returned to the argument that the privilege was guaranteed against State abridgment as a privilege of national—and not merely State—citizenship. This is what Justice Moody wrote:

> Much might be said in favor of the view that the privilege was guaranteed against state impairment as a privilege and immunity of national citizenship, but, as has been shown, the decisions of this court have foreclosed that view.

This was a rather weak, if not apologetic, defense of the precedents. A future Court would not feel itself to be bound by Justice Moody's arguments and the Court's decision in *Twining* v. *New Jersey*.[22]

Justice Harlan, as he had done in previous dissenting opinions, looked backward into constitutional history, and forward into foreseeable dangers were the Court's decision to remain unchallenged.

There could be no doubt, he said, that, as the Fifth Amendment makes clear, immunity from self-incrimination was one of the privileges or immunities belonging to American citizens. This was the case in 1868 when the Fourteenth Amendment was adopted. Now, this amendment expressly forbids any State from making or enforcing a law that will abridge the privileges or immunities of American citizens, or deprive any person of life, liberty, or property without due process of law. It follows, therefore, that

> The privileges and immunities in the original Amendments, and universally regarded as our heritage of liberty from the common law, were thus secured to every citizen of the United States, and placed beyond assault by any government, Federal or state; and due process of law, in all public proceedings affecting life, liberty, or property, was enjoined equally upon the nation and the state.

Justice Harlan went on to say that he would not attempt to enumerate "all the privileges and immunities which *at that time* [1868] belonged to citizens of the United States";[23] he could, however, "confidently assert" that among them was the privilege of immunity from self-incrimination, which the people had written into the Fifth Amendment. It was his belief, he said, that the Fourteenth Amendment would have been disapproved if it had excluded the guarantee against self-incrimination; for it is "common knowledge that the compelling of a person to criminate himself shocks or ought to shock the sense of right and justice to everyone who loves liberty."

Justice Harlan said that as he read the Court's opinion, it would follow from its underlying general principles and its reasoning that the Fourteenth Amendment would not stand in the way of a State resorting to such cruel and unusual punishments as the thumb screw or the rack; or to infringing the right of free speech; or to authorizing unreasonable searches or seizures, or to putting an accused person in double jeopardy. He concluded by stating that he could not support "any judgment declaring that immunity from self-incrimination is not one of the privileges or immunities of national citizenship, nor a part of the liberty guaranteed by the Fourteen Amendment against hostile state action."

The opinion by Justice Harlan in *Twining* left the Court with various options to move in the future along one or another line of thought.

There is language in his opinion to support (a) a theory of "incorporation" of the first eight amendments into the Fourteenth Amendment; (b) a theory of "selective incorporation"; (c) a doctrine of fundamental rights—rights so basic and essential that their abridgment "ought to shock the sense of right and justice to everyone who loves liberty"; (d) reliance on the Citizenship and Privileges or Immunities Clauses of the Fourteenth Amendment; or (e) reliance on the Due Process Clause of the Fourteenth Amendment.

As we shall see, each of these approaches, except for (d), has played a prominent role in the constitutional history of the twentieth century, especially the doctrine of fundamental rights, based on the concept of liberty guaranteed by the Due Process Clause.

Notes

1. *Slaughter-House Cases*, 16 Wall (83 U.S.) 36 (1873).
2. *Walker* v. *Sauvinet*, 92 U.S. 90 (1876).
3. *United States* v. *Cruikshank*, 92 U.S. 542 (1876). Justice Nathan Clifford wrote a concurring opinion; there were no dissents.
4. *Hurtado* v. *California*, 110 U.S. 516 (1884) Justice Field did not participate in the case.
5. *Presser* v. *Illinois*, 116 U.S. 252 (1886).
6. *Ex parte Spies*, 123 U.S. 131 (1887).
7. The opinion cited on this point *Barron* v. *Baltimore*, 32 U.S. 243, decided in 1833, years before the adoption of the Fourteenth Amendment, and also the more recent cases of *United States* v. *Cruikshank*, *Walker* v. *Sauvinet*, and *Ex parte Presser*.
8. See *The Constitution of the United States of America*, Congressional Research Service, Library of Congress (Washington, D.C., 1987), 952.
9. Both these Justices participated in the *Spies* case but they did not dissent, perhaps out of respect for the principle of *stare decisis*, though the logic of their earlier dissents should have led them to agree with the position of counsel for the defendant.
10. *Ex parte Kemmler*, 136 U.S. 436 (1890).
11. *McElvaine* v. *Brush*, 142 U.S. 155 (1891).
12. *O'Neil* v. *Vermont*, 144 U.S. 323 (1892).
13. *Barron* v. *Baltimore*, 32 U.S. 243 (1833).
14. Justice David J. Brewer joined in the dissenting opinion of Justice Harlan.
15. *Maxwell* v. *Dow*, 176 U.S. 581 (1900).
16. Ibid.
17. *Callan* v. *Wilson*, 127 U.S. 540 (1888); *Thompson* v. *Utah*, 170 U.S. 343 (1898).
18. See *Wilkerson* v. *Utah*, 99 U.S. 130, 135 (1878); *Louisiana ex rel. Francis* v. *Resweber*, 329 U.S. 459 (1947).
19. See *Duncan* v. *Louisiana*, 391 U.S. 145 (1968).
20. *McCulloch* v. *Maryland*, 17 U.S. 316, 407 (1819).
21. *Twining* v. *New Jersey*, 211 U.S. 78 (1908).

22. *Twining* v. *New Jersey* was overruled by *Malloy* v. *Hogan,* 378 U.S. 1 (1964).
23. Italics in original.

4

Where Do We Find
Fundamental Rights?

I.

As we have seen, in *Twining* v. *New Jersey*[1] Justice Moody, in his opinion for the Court, left the door open for future constitutional developments which might gradually define the essentials of the claims asserted by Justice Washington and certain dissenting Justices, most notably Justices Field, Bradley, and Harlan. Justice Moody observed, almost marginally, that

> it is possible that some of the personal rights safeguarded by the first eight amendments against national action may also be safeguarded against state action, because a denial of them would be a denial of due process. . . . If this is so, it is not because those rights are enumerated in the first eight amendments, but because they are of such nature that they are included in the conception of due process of law.

This turned out to be a prophetic statement. In due time, the stone which the Court rejected became the chief cornerstone. The resulting doctrine, at the end of a long and tortuous line of development, came to be based on the Due Process Clause of the Fourteenth Amendment, on the "incorporation" of some but not all of the first eight amendments, on the Ninth Amendment,[2] and on the "penumbras, formed by emanations from those guarantees that help give them [i.e., the guarantees] life and substance."[3] The line of development was by no means a straight and easy one; the Court was often divided, the debates were often passionate and vehement, and the members of the Court at times

61

seemed to be uncertain as they sought for a constitutional principle into which to anchor their conclusions.

In 1923, fifteen years after the decision in *Twining*, the Court opened a new chapter in constitutional history with its decision in *Meyer* v. *Nebraska*.[4] The decision and opinion in this case may be said to mark the beginning of the modern period. While all of the cases we have previously discussed have an historical importance, *Meyer* v. *Nebraska* continues to have living significance and to enjoy a distinguished place in any discussion of the idea of fundamental rights.

During and immediately after World War I some State legislatures and local school boards sought to prohibit the teaching of the German language. In some instances the prohibition had a special impact on Lutheran parochial schools, which used German extensively in their teaching program. The Nebraska statute, which was before the Court in *Meyer*, forbade the teaching, in any public or private school, of any subject except in English; it also forbade the teaching of any modern language until the pupil had passed the eighth grade.

In his opinion for the Court, Justice James C. McReynolds[5] said that

> The problem for our determination is whether the statute . . . unreasonably infringes the liberty guaranteed to the plaintiff in error [a teacher of German in a parochial school] by the 14th Amendment. "No state . . . shall deprive any person of life, liberty, or property without due process of law."

This statement of the issue introduces no question about the application of any one of the first eight amendments to State action; nor does it challenge the Nebraska statute as an abridgment of the Privileges or Immunities Clause of the Fourteenth Amendment. The issue as restated by the Court seems to have taken its cue and direction from the statement quoted above from Justice Moody's opinion in *Twining*.

What is the liberty guaranteed by the Fourteenth Amendment? Without attempting to define the term with exactness, the Court said that "without doubt" the term includes the following:

> freedom from bodily restraint,
> the right of the individual to contract,
> to engage in any of the common occupations of life,
> to acquire useful knowledge,
> to marry,
> establish a home and bring up children,
> to worship God according to the dictates of his own conscience,

and, generally, to enjoy those privileges long recognized at common law as essential to the orderly pursuit of happiness by free men.

At one point in the Court's opinion the stress seemed to have been on "the right of an individual to contract," for the Court said that the defendant's "right thus to teach and the right of parents to engage him so to instruct their children [in a private school], we think, are within the liberty of the Amendment." But the Court also gave a much broader rationale for its decision:

> The legislature has attempted materially to interfere with the calling of modern language teachers [an interference with the right to engage in any of the common occupations of life], with the opportunities of pupils to acquire knowledge [the right to acquire useful knowledge], and with the powers of parents to control the education of their own [the right to establish a home and bring up children].

While the State "may do much," wrote the Court, "*the individual has certain fundamental rights which must be respected.*"[6] Anticipating by a half-century the Federal Government's interest in bi-lingual education, the Court said, "The protection of the Constitution extends to all—to those who speak other languages as well as to those born with English on the tongue."

There is not much explicit constitutional theory in the opinion, but in the light of the earlier cases which we have discussed, it is not difficult to infer the theoretical underpinnings derived from the opinion in *Corfield* and the dissenting opinions in *Slaughter-House* and subsequent decisions. We now, in *Meyer*, have a case in which the Court, by 7–2 vote,[7] decided that the liberty guaranteed to persons by the Due Process Clause includes a person's fundamental rights, which the State must protect.

Two years later, in 1925, the Court had before it *Pierce* v. *Society of Sisters*.[8] Oregon by statute prohibited parochial and private schools for children between the ages of eight and sixteen, by requiring their attendance only at public schools. The Supreme Court unanimously held the statute unconstitutional. Again writing the opinion for the Court, Justice McReynolds pointed out that the Roman Catholic parochial school and the private military academy which brought the action challenging the statute, had important property and contract interests at stake, and that the inevitable result of enforcement of the act would be the destruction of these schools. These parties were engaged "in a kind of undertaking not inherently harmful, but long regarded as useful and meritorious." This language in the opinion implies that, as in *Meyer,* the Court here was, in part, upholding the right of a person "to engage in any of the common occupations of life"—the right to establish and conduct a school (subject to reasonable regulation by the State). But the Court went beyond this proposition, to assert boldly that

> The fundamental theory of liberty upon which all governments in this Union repose excludes any general power of the state to standardize its children by forcing them to accept instruction from public teachers only. The child is not the mere creature of the state; those who nurture him and direct his destiny have the right, coupled with the high duty, to recognize and prepare him for additional obligations.

In making this point, the Court was once again stressing the constitutional status of the family, for in *Meyer,* Justice McReynolds attempted to dissociate the American family institution from certain radically different forms. By way of contrast, he referred to the arrangement in Plato's *Republic,* in which wives of the guardians and their children are held in common, so that no parent knows his or her own child, nor any child his or her parents; and the example of Sparta, where boys, at the age of seven, were placed in barracks, where they were taught and trained by "official guardians." Although men of great genius have approved such measures, "their ideas touching the relation between individual and state were wholly different from those upon which our institutions rest; and it hardly will be affirmed that any legislature could impose such restrictions upon the people of a state without doing violence to both letter and spirit of the Constitution."

But it should be noted that in neither of these cases did the Court base its decision on any "letter" of the Constitution, except the concept of "liberty," as the term is used in the Due Process Clause. No attempt was made to refer back to any one of the first eight amendments. The Court simply explicated the term "liberty" to include certain "fundamental rights," among them the "liberty" to acquire useful knowledge (such as a modern foreign language), the "liberty" of parents to educate their children in private or parochial schools, and the "liberty" to engage in the common occupations of life (such as teaching German or conducting a private or parochial school). These cases, precisely because they were not anchored in the Bill of Rights or in any "letter" of the Constitution other than the undefined—and ultimately indefinable—term "liberty," years later served as useful precedents and guides for the Court protecting liberties and rights that reflect the "spirit of the Constitution."

In brief, what we find in the *Meyer* and *Pierce* cases is the idea or principle that the term "liberty" in the Due Process Clause may have its own generative power and stand on its own ground without dependence on the specific liberties guaranteed by the Bill of Rights. How far-reaching or confined that "liberty" is will be defined on a case-by-case basis. As these two cases illustrate, the term is not confined exclusively to the guarantees of the Bill of Rights.

II.

At the very same time that the Court decided the *Pierce* case, that, together with *Meyer*, began one significant line of development which flowed into the doctrine of fundamental rights, it also decided the *Gitlow* case,[9] that began another equally significant line of development which has contributed heavily to the fundamental rights doctrine. Taken together, this trilogy of cases occupies a place of preeminence in constitutional history.

In *Gitlow* v. *New York* the Supreme Court, in 1925, sustained a conviction under the New York "criminal anarchy" statute, which prohibited the "advocacy, advising or teaching the duty, necessity or propriety of overthrowing or overturning organized government by force or violence" and the publication or distribution of matter advocating, advising or teaching "the doctrine that organized government should be overthrown by force, violence or any unlawful means." It was contended on behalf of the defendant that the statute contravenes the Due Process Clause of the Fourteenth Amendment—that the "liberty" protected by the amendment "includes the liberty of speech and of the press."

Although the Court upheld the New York statute, Justice Sanford, in his opinion for the majority, made the following statement, which represents a revolutionary break with the past:

> For present purposes we may and do assume that freedom of speech and of the press—which are protected by the First Amendment from abridgment by Congress—are among the fundamental personal rights and "liberties" protected by the due process clause of the Fourteenth Amendment from impairment by the States.

The Court did not argue this point; it made no attempt to give reasons for this proposition, of transcendent importance, which it easily assumed, as if no one had ever questioned it or could possibly do so. The only attempt by Justice Sanford to deal with precedents was a reference to a case decided by the Court only three years before,[10] in which the Court said that "neither the Fourteenth Amendment nor any other provision of the Constitution of the United States imposes upon the States any restrictions about 'freedom of speech' or the 'liberty of silence.'" Justice Sanford characterized this passage in the earlier case as an "incidental statement" (which it was) that was not "determinative" of the question before the Court in *Gitlow*.

The Court in *Gitlow* thus took one broad, breathtaking leap, making a decision that was to have the most significant consequences for constitutional development and for the American people and its institutions. What dissenting Justices had urged upon the Court for years now became the position of the entire Court.[11] "I go further and hold," wrote Justice Harlan in a dissenting opinion eighteen years before *Gitlow*, "that the privileges of free speech and a free press, belonging to every citizen of the United States, constitute essential parts of every man's liberty, and are protected against violation by that clause of the Fourteenth Amendment forbidding a state to deprive any person of his liberty without due process of law."[12]

In 1927, two years after *Gitlow*, Justice Brandeis uncovered the basic, far-reaching principle on which Justice Sanford's statement was based. Justice Brandeis wrote in a concurring opinion in *Whitney* v. *California*:[13]

> Despite arguments to the contrary which had seemed to me persuasive, it is settled that the due process clause of the Fourteenth Amendment applies to matters of substantive law as well as to matters of procedure. *Thus all fundamental rights comprised within the term liberty are protected by the Federal Constitution from invasion by the States.* The right of free speech, the right to teach and the right of assembly are, of course, fundamental rights. . . . These may not be denied or abridged. . . .

In due course, in case by case, the Court selected certain rights as *fundamental* and placed them under the protection of the Fourteenth Amendment's guarantee of *liberty*. This was the *substantive* due process to which Justice Brandeis had originally objected but to which he became reconciled when not used to strike down laws regulating business and industrial conditions.

The terms "liberty" and "due process of law," as used in the Four-teenth Amendment, are no longer inextricably connected. Each has substantially a life of its own. The amendment has come to mean, not simply that one may not be deprived of his *liberty without due process*, but that one is guaranteed substantive *liberty*, and that one is also guaranteed *procedural due process*. In one of the school desegregation cases of 1954,[14] the Supreme Court said:

> Although the Court has not assumed to define "liberty" with great precision, that term is not confined to mere freedom from bodily restraint [as the term "liberty" was used at common law[15]]. Liberty under law extends to the full range of conduct which the individual is free to pursue, . . .

What that "full range of conduct" encompasses no one can say, for it is an open-ended concept, but beginning with *Meyer, Pierce,* and *Gitlow,* the Court has charted out an impressive list of fundamental rights that are included in the guarantee of liberty as substantive or procedural due process.[16]

III.

In the famous *Scottsboro* case[17] before the Supreme Court in 1932 the issue was whether the guarantee of the Sixth Amendment to the right to have counsel for one's defense applies to a State's criminal prosecution. Nine Negroes were charged in Alabama with having raped two white girls on a freight train. They were convicted and sentenced to death. On appeal, the Supreme Court found that until the very morning of the trial no lawyer had been named or definitely desig-nated to represent the defendants, who were ignorant, illiterate, not residents of Alabama, and "regarded with especial horror in the com-munity where they were to be tried." The Court held that the defen-dants had not been accorded "the right of counsel in any significant sense." The Court referred to *Hurtado* but, in light of the circum-stances presented in the instant case, thought that the "sweeping char-acter of the language in the *Hurtado* case, the rule laid down is not without exceptions." The fact that the right to counsel involved in the *Scottsboro* case, said the Court,

> is of such a character that it cannot be denied without violating those "fundamental principles of liberty and justice which lie at the base of all our civil and political institutions,"[18] is obviously one of those compelling considerations which must

prevail [despite *Hurtado*] in determining whether it is embraced within the due process clause of the Fourteenth Amendment, although it be specifically dealt with in another part of the federal Constitution. . . . it [is] clear that the right to the aid of counsel is of this fundamental character. . . . To hold otherwise would be to ignore the fundamental postulate . . . "that there are certain immutable principles of justice which inhere in the very idea of free government which no member of the Union may disregard."[19]

The Court in this case, then, did not "incorporate" the Sixth Amendment into the Fourteenth. It looked to it for guidance, instruction, and, to a degree, as a model; but basically the Court interpreted "due process" as including the fundamental principle of justice, the immutable principle of justice, that defendants in a capital case are entitled to assigned counsel "as a necessary requisite of due process." The Court did not go beyond this; it did not hold broadly, as the Sixth Amendment provides, that in *all* criminal prosecutions, the accused shall enjoy the right to have the assistance of counsel for his defense. The test was due process and not the Sixth Amendment's guarantee of the right to have counsel.

The later history of the right to counsel offers a convenient opportunity to pull together the contrasting views regarding the issue of "incorporation" of the first eight amendments into the Fourteenth. There is a great deal of underbrush that will be bypassed as we concentrate on the main developments.

In *Gideon*,[20] decided in 1963, the defendant was charged in a Florida State court with having broken into and entered a poolroom with intent to commit a misdemeanor. This offense was a felony under Florida law. Gideon asked the court to appoint counsel for him, since he was without funds. The judge said that the State was required to appoint counsel only in a capital case; and so Gideon was tried before a jury, before whom he conducted his own defense. He was found guilty and sentenced to serve five years in prison.

When the case came before the Supreme Court, what stood in Gideon's way was the Court's decision, in 1942, in *Betts* v. *Brady*,[21] a case similar to Gideon's on the essential facts, in which the Court held that a refusal to appoint counsel for an indigent defendant charged with a felony did not necessarily violate the Due Process Clause of the Fourteenth Amendment. The Court in *Betts* held that the claimed denial of due process was to be tested by an appraisal of the totality of facts in a given case, for what may be a denial of fairness, "shocking to the universal sense of justice," under one set of facts, may, "in other circumstances, and in the light of other considerations," fall short of being a denial of due process. The test was the broad, fluid concept of due process, and not the specific requirements of the Sixth Amendment.

In *Gideon*, the Supreme Court unanimously overruled *Betts* v. *Brady*. In his opinion for the Court, Justice Black stated that the Court had erred in *Betts* when it concluded that "appointment of counsel is not a fundamental right, essential to a fair trial." Had the Court held that appointment of counsel for an indigent criminal defendant was a fundamental right, "it would have held that the Fourteenth Amendment requires appointment of counsel in a state court, just as the Sixth Amendment requires in a federal court." The Court said that

> the Court in *Betts* had ample precedent for acknowledging that those guarantees of the Bill of Rights which are fundamental safeguards of liberty immune from federal abridgment are equally protected against state invasion by the Due Process Clause of the Fourteenth Amendment.

It is important to note that the Court did not say that all first eight amendments were simply to be read into the Due Process Clause of the Fourteenth Amendment, as having been "incorporated" into it. What the Court said was that "those guarantees of the Bill of Rights which are fundamental safeguards of liberty immune from federal abridgment"—not necessarily *all* guarantees of the Bill of Rights, but *only those that are "fundamental safeguards of liberty"*—are to be taken into the Due Process Clause. First must come the question whether the asserted claim is of a fundamental right, and only if this question is answered in the affirmative do we then reach the conclusion that if it is guaranteed by the Bill of Rights, then that guarantee is "incorporated" into the Fourteenth Amendment. *The primary, basic inquiry is whether the asserted claim is of a fundamental right.*

The Court pointed out that the Court's opinion in *Powell* v. *Alabama* had stated that

> the Fourteenth Amendment "embraced" those "fundamental principles of liberty and justice which lie at the base of all our civil and political institutions."

Justice Black then listed interests that the Court in previous cases had found to be of "this fundamental nature" that are guaranteed by the Bill of Rights and therefore made immune from State invasion by the Fourteenth Amendment. He listed the following fundamental rights:

First Amendment:
  speech[22]
  press[23]
  religion[24]
  assembly[25]
  association[26]
  petition[27]
Fourth Amendment:
  against unreasonable searches and seizures[28]
Fifth Amendment:
  private property not to be taken without just compensation[29]
Eighth Amendment:
  ban on cruel and unusual punishment.[30]

It should be noted once more that *Gideon* was decided in 1963. In the four decades between *Gitlow* and *Gideon* the process of "incorporation" spread out, the influence of *Gitlow* radiated, the search for rights or interests that could be considered fundamental continued. Once the process was started, its force could hardly be abated. There could hardly be any question about the fundamental character of the First Amendment rights; even the strong feelings against "substantive due process" after 1937[31] could not stand in the way of the Court giving national character and national protection to rights which it thought no free government could deny to any person. Any other judicial position would have deprived the concept "liberty" in the Fourteenth Amendment of almost all significance. As the second Justice Harlan observed:

> Were due process merely a procedural safeguard it would fail to reach those situations where the deprivation of life, liberty or property was accomplished by [State] legislation which by operating in the future could, given even the fairest possible procedure in application to individuals, nevertheless destroy the enjoyment of all three. . . . [32]

Although the Court's decision in *Gideon* was unanimous, there were three concurring opinions, one of which should claim our attention at this point:

Justice Douglas limited his opinion chiefly to an historical survey which showed that up to *Gideon* ten Justices had taken the stand that the Fourteenth Amendment "incorporated" the Bill of Rights. These Justices were the following:

Field[33]
Harlan (the first)[34]
Brewer[35]
Bradley[36]
Swayne[37]
Clifford[38]
Murphy[39]
Rutledge[40]
Black[41]
Douglas[42]

This summary Justice Douglas put into his opinion, not by way of argument in favor of total incorporation, but only as "a brief historical resume." Indeed, Justice Black, who was the chief proponent of the doctrine that the Fourteenth Amendment took into itself *all* of the Bill of Rights as safeguards against infringement by the States, did not resort to this doctrine in his opinion for the Court in *Gideon*. He contended only that

> those guarantees of the Bill of Rights which are fundamental safeguards of liberty immune from federal abridgment are equally protected against state invasion by the Due Process Clause of the Fourteenth Amendment.

This is, of course, an expression of the doctrine of "selective," not total, "incorporation."

In 1947, in a dissenting opinion in *Adamson* v. *California*,[43] Justice Black argued that the Fourteenth Amendment "incorporates" *all* of the Bill of Rights. He contended that

> history conclusively demonstrates that the language of the first section of the Fourteenth Amendment, taken as a whole, was thought by those responsible for its submission, sufficiently explicit to guarantee that thereafter no state could deprive its citizens of the privileges and protections of the Bill of Rights. . . . I would follow what I believe was the original purpose of the Fourteenth Amendment—to extend to all the people of the nation the complete protection of the Bill of Rights. To hold that this Court can determine what, if any, provisions of the Bill of Rights will be enforced, and if so to what degree is to frustrate the great design of a written Constitution.

In this argument in *Adamson*, Justice Black was joined by Justices Douglas and Murphy, and Justice Wiley B. Rutledge. But the full incorporation argument has not ever won majority approval in the Court, and the accuracy of his historical thesis has been the subject of debate.[44] Justice Black came to support the selective incorporation doctrine as an alternative to total incorporation—as we have seen from his opinion for the Court in *Gideon*—even though, in his view, the selective incorporation doctrine is historically less supportable.

IV.

A passage in the Court's opinion in *Twining*,[45] which we have previously quoted, opened the door to "selective incorporation" as well as to the doctrine of fundamental rights. It was sufficiently ambiguous to allow movement in the direction of either theory. The Court had said that

> it is possible that some of the personal rights safeguarded by the first eight amendments against national action may also be safeguarded against state action, because a denial of them would be a denial of due process. . . . If this is so, it is not because these rights are enumerated in the first eight amendments, but because they are of such nature that they are included in the conception of due process of law.

While the Court has refused to give content to the Due Process Clause by pouring into it the whole of the Bill of Rights, it has not hesitated to consider specific guarantees, on a case by case basis, as giving some meaning to the term due process. The Bill of Rights has thus served as both a source and a guide.

The essential elements of the Court's approach have their chief inspiration in Justice Cardozo's opinions in two cases, to which we now turn.

In the first, and less important, case, *Snyder* v. *Massachusetts*,[46] the question was whether Massachusetts had denied the defendant due process by permitting a view by the jury in the absence of the defendant. The Court held that his presence was not required by due process. In his opinion for the Court, Justice Cardozo said that the State

> is forced to regulate the procedure of its courts in accordance with its own conception of policy and fairness *unless in so doing it offends some principle of justice so rooted in the traditions and conscience of our people as to be ranked as fundamental.*[47]

When tested by this standard, said Justice Cardozo, trial by jury may be abolished consistently with the Fourteenth Amendment; and so, too, indictment by grand jury may give way to information by a public officer; and so, too, the privilege of self-incrimination may be withdrawn. The test for the State, then, is, obviously, not what the Fifth, Sixth, or Seventh Amendments require (as against the Federal Government), but what the Due Process Clause requires of the State. These amendments are not to be read verbatim into the Fourteenth Amendment. What is read into the amendment is that the State's procedure may not be such as will offend "some principles of justice so rooted in the traditions and conscience of our people as to be ranked as fundamental." *Only rights that are fundamental are guaranteed by the Fourteenth Amendment.*

The second—and by far the more important—case was *Palko* v. *Connecticut*,[48] decided in 1937. A statute of Connecticut permitted the State to appeal decisions in criminal cases. The defendant had been convicted of second degree murder. The State appealed, and the Connecticut Supreme Court of Errors reversed on the ground that the trial court had committed errors of law to the prejudice of the State. The defendant was tried again and was found guilty of first degree murder. Defendant contended that his second trial had placed him in double jeopardy for the same offense. The Fifth Amendment contains an immunity from double jeopardy. The argument was that whatever is forbidden by the Fifth Amendment against the Federal Government is forbidden by the Fourteenth Amendment against the States.

In his opinion for the Court affirming the judgment against the defendant, Justice Cardozo explicitly denied that there was a general rule by which the Fourteenth Amendment absorbed the first eight amendments. As he had done in *Snyder*, Justice Cardozo cited cases in which the Court had explicitly refused to apply to a State a specific right or immunity guaranteed by one of the first eight amendments. On the other hand, he noted that the Court had assimilated into the Fourteenth Amendment guarantees of the First Amendment—free speech, freedom of the press, free exercise of religion, peaceable assembly—and also the Sixth Amendment right to have the assistance of counsel. In these latter situations, "immunities that are valid as against the federal government by force of the specific pledges of particular amendments have been found to be *implicit in the concept of ordered liberty*, and thus, through the Fourteenth Amendment, become valid as against the states." In other words, it was not that the States were constitutionally bound by the first eight amendments; they were bound, by the Fourteenth Amendment, to respect the "liberty" of persons, that is, the rights "implicit in the concept of ordered liberty."

There is, said Justice Cardozo, a "rationalizing principle" which divides the cases in which the Court *denied* the application of a specific guarantee of the Bill of Rights to the States and those in which the Court *enforced* specific guarantees of the Bill of Rights against the States. The former guarantees, while they may have value and importance, "are not of the *very essence of a scheme of ordered liberty*. To abolish them is not to violate a '*principle of justice so rooted in the traditions and conscience of our people as to be ranked as fundamental*'." Of them—such as jury trials, grand jury indictments, and immunity from compulsory self-incrimination—it may be said, "This too might be lost, and justice still be done." The latter guarantees, however, are on a "different plane of social and moral values."

> These in their origin were effective against the federal government alone. If the Fourteenth Amendment has absorbed them, *the process of absorption has had its source in the belief that neither liberty nor justice would exist if they were sacrificed.*

At this point the opinion cited *Twining* and quoted the passage from the Court's opinion in that case which we have set forth at the beginning of this section.

Justice Cardozo strongly implied that the Court was rejecting the notion of even "selective incorporation." Referring to the Scottsboro case decision (*Powell* v. *Alabama*), the Court said that the decision in that case

> did not turn upon the fact that the benefit of counsel would have been guaranteed to the defendants by the provisions of the Sixth Amendment if they had been prosecuted in a federal court. The decision turned upon the fact that in the particular situation laid before us in the evidence the benefit of counsel was essential to the substance of a hearing [and hence to the concept of liberty and the concept of due process].

The question before the Court in *Palko*, Justice Cardozo said, was whether the new trial was the kind of double jeopardy that subjected the defendant to "a hardship so acute and shocking that our polity will not endure it? Does it violate those 'fundamental principles of liberty and justice which lie at the base of all our civil and political institutions?'" "The answer surely must be 'no'."

V.

The unifying principle uncovered by *Palko* is, of course, the concept of fundamental rights. The provisions of the Bill of Rights are not necessarily controlling on the States. Only what is "implicit in the concept of ordered liberty," only that which is "so rooted in the traditions and conscience of our people as to be ranked as fundamental," is a limit on the powers of the States. The first eight amendments may or may not be, in so far as concerns the States, formulations of such fundamental rights. Before Justice Cardozo, Justice Moody had sketched out this approach in *Twining* in 1908, and each of these Justices spoke for the Court.

But before long the *Twining/Palko* approach was under attack, and particularly, as we have seen, by Justice Black in his dissenting opinion in *Adamson*, and in due time it was rejected by the Court in the administration of Chief Justice Warren, and its status in the Burger Court was blurred. It would be tiresome and unprofitable to trace its fortunes in detail through the litigation of the past sixty years; it will suffice for our purpose to select for discussion several typical steps in the uneven line of development. But the Cardozo approach has been vindicated.

Rochin v. *California*,[49] decided in 1952, involved a conviction for illegal possession of morphine. As police officers entered his home, the defendant swallowed two capsules of morphine. He was taken to a hospital where, at the direction of a police officer, a doctor forced an emetic solution into his stomach and against his will. Primarily on the evidence so obtained, he was convicted in the State courts.

In his opinion for the Court, Justice Frankfurter followed the approach of Justice Cardozo. He wrote:

> Due process of law is a summarized constitutional guarantee of respect for those personal immunities which, as Mr. Justice Cardozo twice wrote for the Court, are "so rooted in the traditions and conscience of our people as to be ranked as fundamental," *Snyder* v. *Massachusetts,* or are "implicit in the concept of ordered liberty," *Palko* v. *Connecticut.*

With respect to the police action on the defendant, Justice Frankfurter wrote:

> This is conduct that shocks the conscience. . . . convictions cannot be brought about by methods that offend "a sense of justice. . . . "

> On the facts of this case the conviction of the petitioner has been obtained by methods that offend the Due Process Clause.

There is not a word in the Court's opinion about the application of the Fifth Amendment's prohibition of self-incrimination to the Fourteenth Amendment. The decision was simply that the Due Process Clause of the Fourteenth Amendment will not tolerate a conviction based on methods that offended "a sense of justice," or conduct that "shocks the conscience."

Anticipating the attacks on this approach by Justices Black and Douglas[50] in their concurring opinions, Justice Frankfurter disclaimed the charge that the Court was reviving a natural law philosophy. The absence of specific guidelines (e.g., an absolute prohibition on self-incrimination, as in the Fifth Amendment), does not leave the Due Process Clause to the subjective caprices of the Court. "We may not," he said, "draw on our merely personal and private notions. . . . "

> Due process of law . . . is not to be decided as resort to a revival of "natural law." . . . The faculties of the Due Process Clause may be indefinite and vague, but the mode of their ascertainment is not self-willed. In each case "due process of law" requires an evaluation based on a disinterested inquiry pursued in the spirit of science, on a balanced order of facts exactly and fairly stated, on the detached consideration of conflicting claims, . . . on a judgment not ad hoc and episodic but duly mindful of reconciling the needs both of continuity and of change in a progressive society. . . . the Constitution is "intended to preserve practical and substantial rights, not to maintain theories."

While accepting the majority's decision, Justice Black reiterated his position of the *Adamson* dissent that State courts are no less bound by the Fifth Amendment (as well as the others of the first eight amendments) than are the Federal courts, that

> faithful adherence to the specific guaranties in the Bill of Rights insures a more permanent protection of individual liberty than that which can be afforded by the nebulous standards stated by the majority.

Attacking directly a philosophy of fundamental rights, Justice Black asked why, in its search for indices to such rights, should the Court limit itself to looking only to "the community's sense of fair play and decency," the "traditions and conscience of our people," and "those canons of decency and fairness which express the notions of justice of English-speaking people." Why, he asked, should the Court consider "only the notions of English-speaking peoples to determine what are immutable and fundamental principles of justice [?]" He concluded on a highly pessimistic note: "I long ago concluded," he wrote, "that the accordion-like qualities of this philosophy must inevitably imperil all the individual liberty safeguards specifically enumerated in the Bill of Rights."

Justice Douglas, also concurring, noted that not all civilized legal codes recognize the right against self-incrimination. As an original matter, therefore, it might be debatable whether the Fifth Amendment guarantee against such evidence serves the ends of justice. "But the choice was made by the Framers, a choice which sets a standard for legal trials in this country. . . . If it is a requirement of due process for a trial in a federal courthouse, it is impossible for me to say it is not a requirement of due process for a trial in a state courthouse."

Thus the lines between the two sides were clearly drawn in the *Rochin* opinions: either the *Palko/Twining* fundamental rights approach or the "incorporation" approach—"incorporation" in some sense, total or selective.

But this either/or statement puts the matter too sharply. It is a fair statement where the choice is between *Palko* and Justice Black's dissent in *Adamson*, i.e., between fundamental rights and total incorporation. Once, however, incorporation becomes selective, then the guide for selection must be some formulation of the fundamental rights principle, and we are brought back to *Palko/Twining*.

This, in brief, is what happened in the so-called Warren Court, as may be illustrated by *Duncan v. Louisiana*,[51] decided in 1968, when the Court was composed of Chief Justice Warren, and Associate Justices Black, Douglas, Harlan, Brennan, Potter Stewart, Byron White, Abe Fortas, and Thurgood Marshall. The defendant was convicted in Louisiana courts of simple battery, a misdemeanor, punishable by imprisonment for not more than two years and a fine of not more than $300. He demanded a jury trial but this was denied pursuant to Louisiana law which authorizes trial by jury only in cases in which the punishment is imprisonment at hard labor or death. The Supreme Court reversed the judgment by 7 to 2 vote.

In his opinion for the Court, Justice White said that in resolving conflicting claims concerning the meaning of the "spacious language" of the Due Process Clause, "the Court has looked increasingly to the Bill of Rights for guidance; many of the rights guaranteed by the first eight Amendments to the Constitution have been held to be protected against state action by the Due Process Clause of the Fourteenth Amendment."

By what test is it decided that a right guaranteed by the Bill of Rights with respect to Federal criminal proceedings is also protected against State action by the Fourteenth Amendment? Justice White noted that the test has been phrased in a variety of ways—

> The question has been asked whether a right is among those "fundamental principles of liberty and justice which lie at the base of all civil and political institutions," . . . whether it is "basic in our system of jurisprudence," . . . and whether it is "a fundamental right essential to a fair trial."

The Court's conclusion was as follows:

> Because we believe that trial by jury in criminal cases is fundamental to the American scheme of justice, we hold that the Fourteenth Amendment guarantees a right of jury trial in all criminal cases which—were they to be tried in a federal court—would come within the Sixth Amendment's guarantee.

At this point Justice White inserted an important footnote in which he made reference to *Palko*. In that case, he said, the test seemed to be whether a civilized system of justice could be imagined that would not accord the particular protection. From that approach the Court could reach the decision that a jury trial is not "of the very essence of a scheme of ordered liberty." It would be "narrow" or "provincial" to maintain that "a fair and enlightened system of justice" would be impossible without trials by jury. But recent cases, said Justice White, have proceeded

> upon the valid assumption that state criminal processes are not imaginary and theoretical schemes but actual systems bearing virtually every characteristic of the common-law system that has been developing contemporaneously in England and in this country. The question thus is whether given this kind of system a particular procedure is fundamental—whether, that is, a procedure is necessary to an Anglo-American regime of ordered liberty. . . . it might be said that the limitation in question is not necessarily fundamental to fairness in every criminal system that might be imagined but is fundamental in the context of the criminal processes maintained by the American states. . . .
>
> A criminal process which was fair and equitable but used no juries is easy to imagine. . . . Yet no American State has undertaken to construct such a system. . . .

It is clear that the Court in *Duncan* revised the *Palko* approach in serious respects: (1) What is "fundamental" is not to be considered abstractly, in a universal setting, in the light of what might be considered "civilized." Instead, the Court is to consider what is implied in the American context, viewed in the light of American history, American legal institutions. (2) If it is concluded that a right is fundamental "to the American scheme of justice," then the relevant amendment in the Bill of Rights is absorbed into the Fourteenth Amendment. (3) When a provision of the Bill of Rights is absorbed into the Fourteenth, the guarantee operates against the States with the same force and particularity as it does against the Federal Government.

Justice Black wrote a concurring opinion in which Justice Douglas joined. Justice Black reaffirmed the position he outlined in his *Adamson* dissent, that all of the Bill of Rights was "incorporated" into the Fourteenth Amendment; he was, however, "very happy" to support the selective process, by which the Court has made "most of the specific Bill of Rights' protections applicable to the States to the same extent they are applicable to the Federal Government." He has been willing, he said, "to support the selective incorporation doctrine . . . as an alternative, although perhaps less historically supportable than complete incorporation."

Going beyond the argument from history, Justice Black offered a rationale of the selective incorporation process. If used properly, he said, this process

> does limit the Supreme Court in the Fourteenth Amendment field to specific Bill of Rights' protections only and keeps judges from roaming at will in their own notions of what policies outside the Bill of Rights are desirable and what are not. And, most importantly for me, the selective incorporation process has the virtue of having already worked to make most of the Bill of Rights' protections applicable to the States.

The *Duncan* case offered an opportunity to Justice Harlan to formulate, with some precision, his own philosophy with regard to the relation between the Fourteenth Amendment and the Bill of Rights.[52] In time, as we shall see, it proved to be an influential position. In essence, Justice Harlan's position was that of Justice Cardozo in *Palko*. It articulates aspects of constitutionalism which proved to be persuasive to the Burger Court. Justice Harlan's position was summarized in the second paragraph of his long dissenting opinion:

> The States have always borne primary responsibility for operating the machinery of criminal justice within their borders, and adapting it to their particular circumstances. In exercising this responsibility, each State is compelled to conform its

procedures to the requirements of the Federal Constitution. The Due Process Clause of the Fourteenth Amendment requires that those procedures be fundamentally fair in all respects. It does not, in my view, impose or encourage nationwide uniformity for its own sake; it does not command adherence to forms that happen to be old; and it does not impose on the States the rules that may be in force in the federal courts except where such rules are also found to be essential to basic fairness.

Here in brief compass we have the following positions: (a) the Bill of Rights is neither completely nor selectively incorporated into the Fourteenth Amendment; (b) the Due Process Clause requires only that a State's procedures be "fundamentally fair in all respects"; (c) since the Bill of Rights limits the Federal Government, the procedure in State courts may not be the same as that which is found in Federal courts, as long as the former procedure is "fundamentally fair in all respects"; (d) it must be borne in mind that ours is a federal system of government, in which States have primary responsibility for operating the machinery of criminal justice.

In view of the influence Justice Harlan's approach was to have in the post-Warren Court era—apart from its intrinsic intellectual interest—we shall take a closer look at his line of argument:

First of all, Justice Harlan rejected Justice Black's historical argument that the Fourteenth Amendment incorporated the first eight amendments. Furthermore, the very breadth and generality of such terms in the Fourteenth Amendment as "citizenship," "privileges or immunities," "due process of law," "liberty," and "equal protection of the law" suggest that the amendment's authors "did not suppose that the Nation would always be limited to mid-19th century conceptions of 'liberty' and 'due process of law' but that the increasing experience and evolving conscience of the American people would add new 'intermediate premises' [i.e., new specific rules by which the broad concepts of the amendment could be defined and given content]." Justice Harlan therefore rejected the total and the selective incorporation doctrines, but added that the former had, at least, the virtue of inner consistency, which the latter lacks.

The only other method that has internal logic is the following:

That is to start with the words "liberty" and "due process of law" and attempt to define them in a way that accords with American traditions and our system of government. . . . It entails a "gradual process of judicial inclusion and exclusion," seeking, with due recognition of constitutional tolerance for state experimentation and disparity, to ascertain "those immutable principles . . . of free government which no member of the Union may disregard." Due process was not restricted to rules fixed in the past . . . nor did it impose nationwide uniformity in details . . .

To this "gradual process" the Bill of Rights has a twofold relationship: (a) there may be an accidental overlap or parallelism between what the Due Process Clause imposes and some guarantees of the Bill of Rights, and (b) the Bill of Rights may be useful as evidence, at some points, of the content Americans find in the term "liberty" and of American standards of fundamental fairness.

Certainly there are instances where the right guaranteed against the States by the Fourteenth Amendment is one that is also guaranteed against the Federal Government by the Bill of Rights. *"The logically critical thing, however,"*—and this is at the heart of Justice Harlan's analysis—*"was not that the rights had been found in the Bill of Rights, but that they were deemed, in the context of American legal history, to be fundamental."*[53]

This is clearly the line of the *Palko* approach, as well as the position taken by Justice Frankfurter in his opinion for the Court in *Rochin* (with the gloss, from Justice White's footnote in his *Duncan* opinion, that what is "fundamental" is to be decided, not abstractly, but in the context of American history).

Justice Harlan explicitly argued that his approach is identical with that formulated by Justice Cardozo in *Palko*. He pointed to the fact that Justice Cardozo in that case spoke not only for himself but for the Court, which included Chief Justice Hughes and Justices Brandeis and Stone. When Justice Cardozo spoke of the right to trial by jury and of the immunity from prosecution except as the result of an indictment, he said that these rights "may have value," but

they are not of the very essence of a scheme of ordered liberty. To abolish them is not to violate a "principle of justice so rooted in the traditions and conscience of *our people* as to be ranked as fundamental." . . . [Italics added by Justice Harlan.]

Even if it be decided that a certain right—e.g., trial by jury—is fundamental, it should not follow, said Justice Harlan, that what obtains in Federal trials must also obtain in all State trials. In Federal trials it is settled that a jury means a body of twelve persons; but why must this subordinate rule be binding on the States? A "jury of exactly twelve" "is not fundamental to anything: there is no significance except to mystics in the number 12."

The trouble with the majority opinion, said Justice Harlan, is that it selects only some guarantees of the Bill of Rights for incorporation, and it says that they are selected because they are "fundamental," but it turns out that by this term the majority only mean that they are "old," "much praised," and "found in the Bill of Rights." Thus the majority's definition of "fundamental" is circular: a right is guaranteed by the Bill of Rights because it is "fundamental," and it is a "fundamental" right because it is guaranteed by the Bill of Rights.

According to Justice Harlan, the basic question, when the issue of due process is raised in a State criminal case, is whether the defendant was denied "any element of fundamental procedural fairness." This question cannot be answered by reference to only historical consideration, "for due process is an evolving concept and . . . old principles are subject to re-evaluation in light of later experience."

Trial by jury has, of course, its virtues, and Justice Harlan described them; but it also has its defects, and he described them also, and referred to numerous studies of the jury system in the United States and England; and he mentioned that research had shown that in the United States, of all prosecutions for crimes triable by jury, 75 percent were settled by guilty plea, and 40 percent of the remainder were tried by the court without juries.

The majority in *Duncan* said that they would not claim that a criminal trial held before a judge without a jury is for that reason unfair; yet the majority, Justice Harlan pointed out, reversed the conviction without suggesting that this particular trial was in fact unfair.

Justice Harlan concluded with a re-affirmation of the principle of federalism:

> In sum, there is a wide range of views on the desirability of trial by jury, and on the ways to make it most effective when it is used; there is also considerable variation from State to State in local conditions such as the size of the criminal caseload, the ease or difficulty of summoning jurors, and other trial conditions bearing on fairness. We have before us, therefore, an almost perfect example of a situation in which the celebrated dictum of Mr. Justice Brandeis should be invoked. It is, he said, "one of the happy incidents of the federal system that a single courageous State may, if its citizens choose, serve as a laboratory. . . . " This Court, other courts, and the political process are available to correct any experiments in criminal procedure that prove fundamentally unfair to defendants. . . .

VI.

In the following year, 1969, the Court, by 6–2 vote, confronted *Palko* directly and gave it the *coup de grace*. The case was *Benton* v. *Maryland*.[54] The Court, in an opinion by Justice Marshall, reversed the defendant's conviction for larceny on the ground that it violated the guarantee against double jeopardy. "On the merits, we hold," said the Court, "that the Double Jeopardy Clause of the Fifth Amendment is applicable to the States through the Fourteenth Amendment. . . . "

Just as *Duncan* had found that the right of trial by jury in criminal cases was "fundamental to the American scheme of justice," so, too, said Justice Marshall, "we today find that the double jeopardy prohibition of the Fifth Amendment represents a fundamental ideal in our constitutional heritage, and that it should apply to the States through the Fourteenth Amendment. Insofar as it is inconsistent with this holding, *Palko* v. *Connecticut* is overruled." Justice Marshall stated:

> Our recent cases[55] have thoroughly rejected the *Palko* notion that basic constitutional rights can be denied by the States as long as the totality of the circumstances does not disclose a denial of "fundamental fairness." Once it is decided that a particular Bill of Rights guarantee is "fundamental to the American scheme of justice," *Duncan* v. *Louisiana*, the same constitutional standards apply against both the State and Federal Governments. *Palko*'s roots had thus been cut away years ago. We today only recognize the inevitable.
>
> The fundamental nature of the guarantee against double jeopardy can hardly be doubted. . . . Like the right to trial by jury, it is clearly "fundamental to the American scheme of justice." The validity of petitioner's larceny conviction must be judged, not by the watered-down standard enunciated in *Palko*, but under this Court's interpretations of the Fifth Amendment double jeopardy provision.

Justice Harlan, with Justice Stewart joining,[56] dissented. He said that he felt compelled to make some observations on "what can only be regarded as a complete overruling of one of this Court's truly great decisions." The selective incorporation doctrine, he said again, finds no support either in history or in reason. He concluded on a bitter, sad note:

> More broadly, that this Court should have apparently become so impervious to the pervasive wisdom of the constitutional philosophy embodied in *Palko*, and that it should have felt itself able to attribute to the perceptive and timeless words of Mr. Justice Cardozo nothing more than a "watering down" of constitutional rights, are indeed revealing symbols of the extent to which we are weighing anchors from the fundamentals of our constitutional system.

The Court at this time was composed of Chief Justice Warren and Justices Black, Douglas, Harlan, Brennan, Stewart, White, and Marshall. Justice Fortas had resigned about five weeks before the decision in *Benton*. It was a solid "Warren Court" that decided the case, and for whom Justice Marshall's opinion spoke.

As we shall see, however, a good deal of Justice Cardozo's opinion in *Palko* has survived the decision in *Benton*. The voices of Justices Cardozo, Frankfurter, and Harlan continued to be heard and their approach to questions of fundamental rights continues to exert force and influence. But on the question of selective incorporation, the *Palko* position was discarded, and it has been settled that the following guarantees of the first eight amendments have been "selectively absorbed" or "incorporated" into the Fourteenth Amendment as applicable to the States:[57]

First Amendment: freedoms of speech, press, assembly, petition, free exercise of religion, non-establishment of religion, association.

Fourth Amendment: guarantee against unreasonable search and seizure.

Fifth Amendment: guarantee against compulsory self-incrimination; guarantee against double jeopardy; guarantee against taking of private property for public use without just compensation.

Sixth Amendment: right to counsel, to a speedy and public trial; trial before a jury; right to be confronted by witnesses against defendant; right to have compulsory process for obtaining witnesses.

Eighth Amendment: right to be free of cruel and unusual punishments.

VII.

In overruling *Palko*, Justice Marshall wrote too sweepingly. It is one thing to overrule a decision, and quite another to denigrate and condemn the opinion on which that decision was based. For even when the test formulated by Justice Cardozo is used, Justices may still disagree on its application to the facts. In the *Everson* case, all Justices agreed that the First Amendment mandates a prohibition on any "establishment" of religion by a State, but the Justices disagreed among themselves on the question whether the payment of bus fares, out of tax dollars, to students attending religious schools infringed the Establishment Clause. So, too, using the *Palko* test, Justices could disagree among themselves as to whether or not a State's subjecting a defendant to double jeopardy "offends some principle of justice so rooted in

the traditions and conscience of our people as to be ranked as fundamental." Is a prohibition on double jeopardy "implicit in the concept
of ordered liberty?" Must the Court believe that "neither liberty nor
justice would exist if" the prohibition on double jeopardy "were sacrificed?" As the decisions in *Palko* and in *Benton* demonstrate, at one
time the Court could answer these questions one way, and at another
time another way.

I submit that the logic is inescapable: As long as *all* of the guarantees of the Bill of Rights are not "incorporated" into the Fourteenth
Amendment's Due Process Clause, as long as the process of incorporation is through *selection*, the Court must seek to determine whether
or not an asserted right or liberty is or is not *"fundamental"*; it *must*
assume that there is a *hierarchy* of rights and liberties.

And this process of analysis takes us back to *Corfield,* to the Natural Law philosophy of Justices Washington, and Field, and Harlan,
and further back, by many centuries, to Cicero and Stoicism. There is,
however, a difference. The Justices will not profess to seek a universal
proposition, not some sort of "categorical imperative" that would apply to any man anywhere in the world, not an abstract ideal that must
be inherent in the very essence of an ordered liberty; not something
that would be shocking to an abstractly conceived universal sense of
justice. What, instead, the Court would profess to be seeking is an
ideal found in the American heritage or tradition, something inherent
in our constitutional scheme of ordered liberty. The fundamental rights
and liberties are given a local habitation and a local name. Thus the
Justices, as Justice Frankfurter said in *Adamson*, are not "wholly at
large," in their search for what may be "fundamental" rights. They do
not pose as philosophers mapping out a utopia. They are *American*
jurists. Like Justice Black, each carries a copy of the Constitution in
his or her pocket at all times, and they know American history, American law, the American tradition, American institutions and the values
they represent.

Having said this, I still need to go back to the test as formulated by
Justice Cardozo: Those rights are "fundamental" which represent "principles of justice so rooted in the traditions and conscience *of our
people* as to be ranked as fundamental." The decision in *Benton*, not-
withstanding the disclaimer of Justice Marshall, can be understood
only by a re-reading of *Palko*—not the decision but the opinion of
Justice Cardozo.

Notes

1. *Twining* v. *New Jersey*, 211 U.S. 78 (1908).
2. "The enumeration in the Constitution of certain rights shall not be construed to deny or disparage others retained by the people."
3. *Griswold* v. *Connecticut*, 381 U.S. 479, 485 (1965).
4. *Meyer* v. *Nebraska*, 262 U.S. 390 (1923).
5. James C. McReynolds served as Associate Justice from 1914 to 1941. He was a strict constructionist and wrote more opinions finding acts of Congress unconstitutional than any other member of the Court, and became specially known for his opposition to New Deal legislation. His opinions in *Meyer* v. *Nebraska* and in *Pierce* v. *Society of Sisters*, 268 U.S. 510 (1925) stand out as exceptions in his judicial record as an arch conservative.
6. Italics supplied.
7. Justice George Sutherland and Justice Holmes dissented. The latter contended that since reasonable minds may differ as to the wisdom of the Nebraska law, he was "unable to say that the Constitution of the United States prevents the experiment being tried." His dissenting opinion appears in *Bartels* v. *Iowa*, 262 U.S. 404 (1923), a companion case to *Meyer*.
8. *Pierce* v. *Society of Sisters*, 268 U.S. 510 (1925).
9. *Gitlow* v. *New York*, 268 U.S. 652 (1925). Justice Holmes wrote a dissenting opinion in which Justice Brandeis joined.
10. *Prudential Insurance Co.* v. *Cheek*, 259 U.S. 530, 543 (1922).
11. The dissenting opinion by Justice Holmes did not question the proposition that freedom of speech and of the press is included in the liberty guaranteed by the Fourteenth Amendment.
12. *Patterson* v. *Colorado*, 205 U.S. 454 (1907).
13. *Whitney* v. *California*, 274 U.S. 357 (1927). Italics supplied.
14. *Bolling* v. *Sharpe*, 347 U.S. 497 (1954).
15. See C.E. Shattuck, "The True Meaning of the Term 'Liberty'," 4 *Harvard Law Rev.* 365 (1891).
16. The phrase "substantive due process" essentially means a guarantee of a "liberty" (such as free speech) that has little if anything to do with procedure, while "procedural due process" means a guarantee of a procedural right (such as right to counsel). "Substantive due process" are "code words" standing for non-procedural liberty, like the fundamental rights to which Justice Brandeis referred in *Whitney*, note 13 above.
17. *Powell* v. *Alabama*, 287 U.S. 45 (1932). Justices Pierce Butler and McReynolds dissented. See A.K. Chalmers, *They Shall Be Free* (1951); D.T. Carter, *Scottsboro: A Tragedy of the American South* (1969).
18. *Hebert* v. *Louisiana*, 272 U.S. 312 (1926).
19. *Holden* v. *Hardy*, 169 U.S. 336 (1898).
20. *Gideon* v. *Wainwright*, 372 U.S. 335 (1963); see Anthony Lewis, *Gideon's Trumpet* (1964). For Justice Black's view on selective incorporation, cf. *Duncan* v. *Louisiana*, 391 U.S. 145 (1968), concurring opinion.
21. *Betts* v. *Brady*, 316 U.S. 455 (1942).
22. *Gitlow* v. *New York*, 268 U.S. 652 (1925); *Lovell* v. *Griffin*, 303 U.S. 444 (1938); *Staub* v. *Baxley*, 355 U.S. 313 (1958); *Edwards* v. *So. Carolina*, 372 U.S. 229 (1963).
23. *Gitlow* v. *New York* and *Lovell* v. *Griffin*, note 22 above; *Grosjean* v. *American Press Co.*, 297 U.S. 233 (1936).

24. *Cantwell* v. *Connecticut*, 310 U.S. 296 (1940).
25. *DeJonge* v. *Oregon*, 299 U.S. 353 (1937); *Edwards* v. *So. Carolina*, 372 U.S. 229 (1963).
26. *Shelton* v. *Tucker*, 364 U.S. 479 (1960); *Louisiana ex rel Gremillion* v. *NAACP*, 366 U.S. 296 (1961).
27. *Edwards* v. *So. Carolina*, 372 U.S. 229 (1963).
28. *Wolf* v. *Colorado*, 338 U.S. 25 (1949); *Elkins* v. *United States*, 364 U.S. 206 (1960); *Mapp* v. *Ohio*, 367 U.S. 643 (1961).
29. *Chicago B. & O. R. Co.* v. *Chicago*, 166 U.S. 266 (1897); *Smyth* v. *Ames*, 169 U.S. 466 (1898).
30. *Robinson* v. *California*, 370 U.S. 660 (1962).
31. *West Coast Hotel Co.* v. *Parrish*, 300 U.S. 379 (1937).
32. *Poe* v. *Ullman*, 367 U.S. 497 (1961), dissenting opinion.
33. *O'Neil* v. *Vermont*, 144 U.S. 323.(1892); *Slaughter-House Cases*, 83 U.S. 36 (1873); *Walker* v. *Sauvinet*, 92 U.S. 90 (1876).
34. *O'Neil* v. *Vermont*, 144 U.S. 323 (1892); *Twining* v. *New Jersey*, 211 U.S. 78 (1908).
35. *O'Neil* v. *Vermont*, 144 U.S. 323 (1892); but cf. *Maxwell* v. *Dow*, 176 U.S. 581 (1900).
36. *Slaughter-House Cases*, 83 U.S. 36 (1873); *O'Neil* v. *Vermont*, 144 U.S. 323 (1892).
37. *Slaughter-House Cases*, 83 U.S. 36 (1873).
38. *Walker* v. *Sauvinet*, 92 U.S. 90 (1876).
39. *Adamson* v. *California*, 332 U.S. 46 (1947).
40. Idem.
41. Idem.
42. Idem. Also *Poe* v. *Ullman*, 367 U.S. 497 (1961).
43. *Adamson* v. *California*, 332 U.S. 46 (1947).
44. Chas. Fairman, "Does the Fourteenth Amendment Incorporate the Bill of Rights? The Original Understanding," 2 *Stanford Law Rev.* 5 (1949). Cf. Graham, "Our 'Declaratory' Fourteenth Amendment," 7 *Stanford Law Rev.* 3 (1954). J. tenBroek, *Equal Under Law* (New York, 1965).
45. *Twining* v. *New Jersey*, 211 U.S. 78 (1908).
46. *Snyder* v. *Massachusetts*, 291 U.S. 97 (1934).
47. Italics supplied. The decision was 5 to 4.
48. *Palko* v. *Connecticut*, 302 U.S. 319 (1937). The decision was 8 to 1. Italics supplied.
49. *Rochin* v. *California*, 342 U.S. 165 (1952). Justice Minton did not participate.
50. Justices Murphy and Rutledge were no longer on the Court. They both died in 1949. Justice Cardozo died in 1938.
51. *Duncan* v. *Louisiana*, 391 U.S. 145 (1968).
52. Justice Stewart joined in the dissenting opinion. Justice Fortas wrote a brief concurring opinion.
53. Italics supplied.
54. *Benton* v. *Maryland*, 395 U.S. 784 (1969). Justice White wrote a concurring opinion, not relevant to our discussion.
55. The Court cited *Gideon* v. *Wainwright*, 372 U.S. 335 (1963); *Malloy* v. *Hogan*, 378 U.S. 1 (1964); and *Duncan* v. *Louisiana*, 391 U.S. 145 (1968).
56. On some differences between the positions of Justice Harlan and Justice Stewart, see the dissenting opinion of the former, footnote 12, in *Benton*.
57. Annot. 18 L. ed. 2d 1388 (1968), 23 L. ed. 2d 985 (1970).

5

Are There Two Bills of Rights?

I.

In the 1970s one of the most hotly contested constitutional controversies was one that flows out of the incorporation doctrine; that is, assuming that a State is bound by one of the first eight amendments, is it bound in exactly the same way in which the Federal Government is bound? The issue is an old one, going back to at least 1884, when the first Justice Harlan, dissenting in *Hurtado*,[1] contended that due process, within the meaning of the Fifth and Fourteenth Amendments,

> does not import one thing with reference to the powers of the States, and another with reference to the powers of the general government. If particular proceedings conducted under the authority of the general government, and involving life, are prohibited, because not constituting due process of law required by the Fifth Amendment . . . , similar proceedings, conducted under the authority of the State, must be deemed illegal as not being due process of law within the meaning of the Fourteenth Amendment.

While the first Justice Harlan cannot be said to have explicitly proposed incorporation, he can be said to have urged a single Federal-State standard of fundamental rights. In the twentieth century a number of Justices of the pre-Burger Court days contended that even when, under the selective incorporation process, a provision of the Bill of Rights has been held applicable to the States, its meaning, definition or scope can still be different; for in the one case (involving the Federal Government) the amendment itself is the guarantee, while in the other case (involving a State) the guarantee is the Due Process Clause and not the precise wording and meaning of the relevant amendment.

Thus, e.g., in a free speech case decided in 1952,[2] Justice Jackson said in a concurring opinion:

> The assumption of other dissents is that the "liberty" which the Due Process Clause of the Fourteenth Amendment protects against denial by the States is the literal and identical "freedom of speech or of the press" which the First Amendment forbids only Congress to abridge. The history of criminal libel in America convinces me that the Fourteenth Amendment did not "incorporate" the First, that the powers of Congress and of the States over this subject are not of the same dimensions, and that because Congress probably could not enact this [group libel] law it does not follow that the States may not.

In a leading obscenity case, decided in 1957,[3] Justice Harlan wrote:

> In judging the constitutionality of this conviction [for obscenity under a State law] we should remember that our function in reviewing state judgments under the Fourteenth is a narrow one. We do not decide whether the policy of the State is wise, or whether it is based on assumptions scientifically substantiated. We can inquire only whether the state action so subverts the fundamental liberties implicit in the Due Process Clause that it cannot be sustained as a rational exercise of power. . . . The States' power to make printed words criminal is, of course, confined by the Fourteenth Amendment, but only insofar as such power is inconsistent with our concept of "ordered liberty."

In *Bloom* v. *Illinois*,[4] decided in 1968, Justice Fortas joined six other members of the Court in holding that in a State's prosecution for serious criminal contempts, the State is subject to the jury provisions of Article 3 of the Constitution and of the Sixth Amendment, made binding upon the States by the Due Process Clause; but in a concurring opinion contended that the decision should not be read as importing into the due process guarantee all of the ancillary rules incidental to trial by jury in the Federal courts. Justice Fortas made the point that while the Due Process Clause may guarantee a "jury" trial in prosecutions for serious offenses, the term "jury" may mean one thing under the Sixth Amendment and another under the Due Process Clause. "I see no reason whatever," he wrote,

> for example, to assume that our decision today should require us to impose federal requirements such as unanimous verdicts or a jury of 12 upon the States. We may well conclude that these and other features of federal jury practice are by no means fundamental—that they are not essential to due process of law—and that they are not obligatory on the States.

Then Justice Fortas set forth cogently the reasons for a pluralistic approach—historical, analytical, and functional reasons. He said:

> Neither logic nor history nor the intent of the draftsmen of the Fourteenth Amendment can possibly be said to require that the Sixth Amendment or its jury trial provision be applied to the States together with the total gloss that this Court's decisions have supplied. The draftsmen of the Fourteenth Amendment intended what they said, not more or less: that no State shall deprive any person of life, liberty, or property without due process of law. It is ultimately the duty of this Court to interpret, to ascribe specific meaning to this phrase. There is no reason whatever for us to conclude that, in so doing, we are bound slavishly to follow not only the Sixth Amendment but all of its bag and baggage, however securely or insecurely affixed they may be by law and precedent to federal proceedings. To take this course, in my judgment, would be not only unnecessary but mischievous because it would inflict a serious blow upon the principle of federalism. The Due Process Clause commands us to apply its great standard to state court proceedings to assure basic fairness. It does not command us rigidly and arbitrarily to impose the exact pattern of federal proceedings upon the 50 States. . . . Our Constitution sets up a federal union, not a monolith.
>
> . . . While we may believe (and I do believe) that the right of jury trial is fundamental, it does not follow that the particulars of according that right must be uniform. We should be ready to welcome state variations which do not impair—indeed, which may advance—the theory and purpose of trial by jury.

Justice Fortas served on the Court only from 1965 to 1969, while Justice Harlan served for sixteen years, 1955–71, and it was he who persistently and forcefully led the attack on the doctrine of incorporation, total or selective, and especially on the idea that a provision of the Bill of Rights meant precisely the same thing when considered as a requirement of procedural due process under the Fourteenth Amendment that it did as a guarantee in a Federal criminal case. He could find no historical, philosophical, or prudential reason that would justify the single-rule approach. He put his argument perhaps most cogently in his dissenting opinion in *Duncan* v. *Louisiana*:[5]

> If the problem is to discover and articulate the rules of fundamental fairness in criminal proceedings, there is no reason to assume that the whole body of rules developed in this Court constituting Sixth Amendment jury trial must be required as a unit [in both Federal and State courts]. The requirement of trial by jury in federal criminal cases has given rise to numerous subsidiary questions respecting the exact scope and content of the right. It surely cannot be that every answer the Court has given, or will give, to such a question is attributable to the Founders; or even that every rule announced carries equal conviction of this Court; still less can it be that every such subprinciple is equally fundamental to ordered liberty.

In view of later developments in the Court, the paragraph immediately following the above passage is especially significant:

> Examples abound. I should suppose it obviously fundamental to fairness that a "jury" means an "impartial jury." I should think it equally obvious that the rule, imposed long ago in the federal courts, that "jury" means "jury of exactly twelve," is not fundamental to anything: there is no significance except to mystics in the number 12. Again, trial by jury has been held to require a unanimous verdict of jurors in the federal courts, although unanimity has not been found essential to liberty in Britain, where the requirement has been abandoned.

Justice Stewart often joined Justice Harlan's dissenting opinions attacking the incorporation doctrine, but it is not altogether clear that Justice Stewart consistently objected to the rule that once a guarantee of the Bill of Rights has been absorbed by the Fourteenth Amendment, the provision of the Bill of Rights applied to the States in all respects exactly as it did to criminal procedure in the Federal courts. Each of these Justices has called attention to the fact that they have not always been in complete agreement.[6] But on balance, it would appear that Justice Stewart's name may be associated with Justices Jackson, Harlan, and Fortas on this issue, which, as is apparent, is one that antedates the Burger Court.

II.

A key case will illustrate the issue and make it possible to see it as one that has not been created by the Burger Court.

When *Williams* v. *Florida*[7] was decided in 1970, of the nine members of the Court, only two had been appointed by President Nixon: Chief Justice Burger and Justice Blackmun, but the latter did not participate in the case. Essentially, then, it was still the "Warren Court," but with a new Chief Justice.

Prior to his trial for robbery in a Florida State court, Williams filed a pretrial motion to impanel a 12-person jury instead of the six-person jury provided by Florida law in all but capital cases. The motion was denied by the State courts. Williams was then tried, and upon conviction was sentenced to life imprisonment. With only Justice Marshall dissenting, the judgment of conviction was affirmed by the Supreme Court.

Justice White, in his opinion for the Court, recognized the fact that only two years before, in *Duncan* v. *Louisiana*,[8] it was held that the

Fourteenth Amendment guarantees a right to trial by jury "in all criminal cases that—were they to be tried in a federal court—would come
within the Sixth Amendment's guarantee." Williams' trial for robbery,
"clearly falls within the scope of that holding." Granting that Williams
was entitled to a trial by jury,

> [T]he question in this case then is whether the constitutional guarantee of a trial by
> "jury" necessarily requires trial by exactly 12 persons, rather than some lesser
> number—in this case six. We hold that the 12-man panel is not a necessary ingre-
> dient of trial by jury and that respondent's refusal to impanel more than the six
> members provided for by Florida law did not violate petitioner's Sixth Amend-
> ment rights as applied to the States through the Fourteenth.

This was exactly the point that had been anticipated by Justice Fortas
two years before in his concurring opinion in *Bloom* v. *Illinois*.[9]

Justice White reviewed the history of the jury as an institution, and
pointed out that Lord Coke's explanation of why the number 12 became fixed was "typical"—the *"number of twelve,"* said Coke, "is
much respected in *holy writ*, as 12 *apostles*, 12 *stones*, 12 *tribes*, etc."
The number 12 became fixed in the fourteenth century, said Justice
White, and was simply a "historical accident, unrelated to the great
purposes which gave rise to the jury in the first place." This "accidental feature" of the jury ought not to be held to have been "immutably
codified into our Constitution." The Court's opinion noted that prior
decisions of the Court, in 1898 and 1905, had held that every feature
of the jury as it existed at common law, including the 12-person feature, was necessarily included in the Constitution wherever it referred
to a "jury," whether the feature was essential or only incidental to the
institution.

After reviewing historical documents relating to "the intent of the
Framers," the Court said:

> We do not pretend to be able to divine precisely what the word "jury" imported to
> the Framers, the First Congress, or the States in 1789. It may well be that the usual
> expectation was that the jury would consist of 12. . . . But there is absolutely no
> indication in "the intent of the Framers" of an explicit decision to equate the
> constitutional and common-law characteristics of the jury.

The relevant inquiry, then, is into "the function that the particular
feature [i.e., the 12-person jury] performs and its relation to the purposes of the jury trial. Measured by this standard, the 12-man requirement cannot be regarded as an indispensable component of the Sixth

Amendment." But what is the function—the purpose of the jury? The Court answered this question by saying that

> the essential feature of a jury obviously lies in the interposition between the accused and his accuser of the commonsense judgment of a group of laymen, and in the community participation and shared responsibility that results from that group's determination of guilt or innocence. The performance of this role is not a function of the particular number of the body that makes up the jury.

Although there are dicta in the opinion of Justice White that the rationale would apply also to a six-person jury in Federal cases, the Court's decision was not so sweeping:

> . . . we conclude that petitioner's Sixth Amendment rights, as applied to the States through the Fourteenth Amendment, were not violated by Florida's decision to provide a six-man rather than a 12-man jury.

In his concurring opinion, Justice Harlan pointed out that the "necessary consequence of this decision is that 12-member juries are not *constitutionally* required in federal criminal trials either."[10] If the Court intends this consequence, then, said Justice Harlan, he could not agree, for that would mean "diluting constitutional protections within the federal system itself. . . . " The case demonstrated to Justice Harlan, as was true also of *Duncan*, that at least in the area of criminal procedure "the incorporation doctrine does not fit well with our federal structure." The meaning of the Sixth Amendment, in its application to Federal cases, should be anchored only in history, for the provisions of the Constitution were framed in the language of the English common law "'and are to be read in the light of its history.'" The right to a trial by jury "has no enduring meaning apart from historical form."

With regard to the number 12, as to this, too, history should be decisive, otherwise why should a State conclude that six members would suffice to fulfill the purpose of the jury, why not three? The Court provides no standard.

If selective incorporation is to apply, then the Federal right must apply to the States "'jot-for-jot and case-for-case,'" but then the reality of federalism must be circumvented; for one cannot incorporate the Sixth Amendment into the Fourteenth and give it a different meaning in its application to the States—unless one would reverse the logic and apply to *Federal* cases the *new* meaning contrived for the Sixth Amendment. Justice Harlan would, of course, have scrapped entirely the incorporation doctrine and have proceeded along the line laid out in *Palko*[11]—a "due process" approach "that considers each particular case on its own bottom to see whether the right alleged is one 'implicit in the concept of ordered liberty'." He also contended that

> Flexibility for experimentation in the administration of justice should be returned to the States here and in other areas that now have been swept into the rigid mold of "incorporation." . . .
>
> It is time, I submit, for this Court to face up to the reality implicit in today's holdings and reconsider the "incorporation" doctrine before its leveling tendencies further retard development in the field of criminal procedure by stifling flexibility in the States. . . . [12]

Justice Black, with Justice Douglas joining, concurred and said that the Court's decision did not dilute the Sixth Amendment but was the consequence of the duty to re-examine prior decisions. The prior cases were based on an improper interpretation of the Sixth Amendment. The incorporation doctrine still substantially means that the specific provisions of the Bill of Rights are fully applicable to the States under the same standards that are applied in Federal cases. In other words, according to this view, the Court in *Williams* merely re-examined the definition of "jury" as the term was used in the Sixth Amendment. Having decided that the term did not encompass the number 12, then the Sixth Amendment, as it applies to the Federal Government, or to the States through incorporation into the Fourteenth Amendment, permits the use of the six-person jury in criminal cases.[13]

Justice Marshall, the sole dissenter, took the position that the long line of precedents that, for over seventy years, had held that the Sixth Amendment meant a 12-member jury, ought not to be overruled, and furthermore, that the *same* "trial by jury" is guaranteed to State defendants by the Fourteenth Amendment as to Federal defendants by the Sixth. Quoting from a Supreme Court case decided only in the previous year,[14] Justice Marshall wrote:

> Once it is decided that a particular Bill of Rights guarantee is "fundamental to the American scheme of justice" [*Duncan* v. *Louisiana*], the same constitutional standards apply against both the State and Federal Governments.

The case was decided, as we have noted, in 1970, when seven of the eight participating members of the Court were Justices who had been members of the Warren Court. Yet it was this case, *Williams* v. *Florida*, that began the reexamination of the definition of those fundamental rights that one finds enumerated explicitly in the Bill of Rights and that have relevance in the criminal law process. The main lines taken by members of the Court may be summarized as follows:

Justice White for the Court: The earlier decisions that defined trial by jury, as the phrase stood in the Sixth Amendment, to mean a trial by a 12-member jury, had been wrongly decided. The Sixth Amendment guarantee is satisfied by a six-member jury in trials in State courts under the Fourteenth Amendment as it incorporates the Sixth.

Justice Harlan: The requirement of a 12-member jury in Federal cases is justified by history and precedents. The Fourteenth Amendment does not incorporate the Sixth Amendment; therefore, the 12-member jury requirement does not apply to States; what does apply is the due process approach; the six-member jury satisfies the due process guarantee. Justice Stewart substantially agreed with Justice Harlan.

Justice Black: The incorporation doctrine applies—the Fourteenth Amendment is to be read as incorporating the jury guarantee of the Sixth Amendment, and the guarantee is identical for the States as for the Federal courts; but the Court is not foreclosed from a reconsideration of precedents and history to discover what the Constitution meant by trial by "jury." Such reconsideration leads to the conclusion that the term "jury" in the Sixth Amendment can encompass the six-member jury. Justice Douglas joined in this concurring opinion.

Justice Marshall: There was no historical or other flaw in the earlier cases which held that the Sixth Amendment meant a trial by a 12-person jury. These cases should not be overruled. Since the Sixth Amendment is incorporated into the Fourteenth, only a 12-member jury will satisfy the guarantee of due process against the States.

As we will see, these lines of thought and approach, laid out in 1970 by the Warren Court, continued into the remainder of the decade by what soon became the Burger Court as Justices Powell and Rehnquist, replacing Justices Black and Harlan, joined Chief Justice Burger and Justice Blackmun, later joined by Justice Stevens, who replaced Justice Douglas.

III.

The case which we have chosen to typify the direction taken by the Court following its decision in *Williams* v. *Florida* is *Apodaca* v. *Oregon*,[15] decided in 1972, when the Court had on it the four members appointed by President Nixon and five who had been members of the Warren Court.

Oregon's constitution authorized verdicts by ten of twelve jurors (i.e., non-unanimous verdicts) in criminal cases, except for first-degree murder verdicts. The defendants in *Apodaca* contended that this State law violated the right to trial by jury specified by the Sixth Amendment and made applicable to the States by the Fourteenth Amendment. The Oregon courts rejected this contention and affirmed the convictions. By 5–4 vote the Supreme Court affirmed. The division was such that the Warren Court Justices, dissenting, constituted one camp, except for Justice White, who joined the four Nixon appointees to make a bare majority of five, with Justice White writing the opinion for himself, Chief Justice Burger, and Justices Blackmun and Rehnquist—an opinion for only four of the Justices; Justice Powell, the fifth member who comprised the majority, wrote a separate opinion. In all there were six opinions in the case, articulating the variety of views as to incorporation with which we have already become familiar.

Justice White in the plurality opinion noted that it was in the latter half of the fourteenth century that it became settled that a verdict had to be unanimous. In America unanimity became the accepted rule in the eighteenth century, as Americans, having become more familiar with details of the common law, adopted these details. But, as in *Williams*, the Court took the position that one should not assume that all the features of the common law jury were necessarily preserved in the Constitution. Finding the history of the framing of the Sixth Amendment ambiguous and inconclusive as to the requirement of unanimity, the Court said that it has the duty to consider what is meant by the concept "jury" and determine "whether a feature commonly associated with it is constitutionally required." For this determination the Court had to turn to other than historical considerations.

Considering the function of the jury in contemporary society, the Court reiterated what it had said in *Williams*; namely, that the essential feature of the jury lies "in the interposition between the accused and his accuser of the commonsense judgment of a group of laymen." From this standpoint, said the Court,

A requirement of unanimity . . . does not materially contribute to the exercise of this commonsense judgment. . . . In terms of this function we perceive no difference between juries required to act unanimously and those permitted to convict or acquit by votes of 10 to two or 11 to one.

The defendants argued that the requirement of unanimity gives substance to the reasonable-doubt standard required by the Due Process Clause. This contention, it should be noted, implies that the Due Process Clause is "incorporated" into the Sixth Amendment—the reverse process to that involved in the incorporation doctrine as formulated by Justice Black[16] and as generally understood.[17] The Court met this contention by reference to history:

> We are quite sure . . . that the Sixth Amendment itself has never been held to require proof beyond a reasonable doubt in criminal cases. The reasonable doubt standard developed separately from both the jury trial and the unanimous verdict. . . . The rule requiring proof of crime beyond a reasonable doubt did not crystallize in this country until after the Constitution was adopted.[18]

Justice Powell, concurring,[19] contended that the concept of jury trial as applicable to States under the Fourteenth Amendment is not identical in all details to the concept required in Federal courts by the Sixth Amendment. An unbroken line of cases have held that unanimity is one of the indispensable features of Federal jury trial,

> not because unanimity is necessarily fundamental to the function performed by the jury, but because the result is mandated by history. . . . At the time the Bill of Rights was adopted, unanimity had long been established as one of the attributes of a jury conviction at common law. It therefore seems to me, in accord both with history and precedent, that the Sixth Amendment requires a unanimous jury verdict to convict in a federal criminal trial.

Since it is the Fourteenth Amendment that provides the test for the States, what Justice Fortas said in his concurring opinion in *Duncan* becomes relevant, and Justice Powell quoted from that opinion as follows:

> I see no reason whatever . . . to assume that our decision today would require us to impose federal requirements such as unanimous verdicts on a jury of 12 upon the States. . . .

Justice Douglas in his dissenting opinion, in which Justices Brennan and Marshall joined, reiterated his view that the concept of "jury" is determined by the Sixth Amendment as to both Federal and State trials, that the Fourteenth Amendment does not guarantee merely "watered-down" versions of the guarantees of the Bill of Rights, that the standards commanded by the Bill of Rights as to Federal trials have been held, by previous cases, to be fully enforceable against the States.[20] These precedents ought not to be tampered with. Justice Douglas said:

> The requirements of a unanimous jury verdict in criminal cases and proof beyond a reasonable doubt are so embedded in our constitutional law and touch so directly all the citizens and are such important barricades of liberty that if they are to be changed they should be introduced by constitutional amendment. . . .
>
> The vast restructuring of American law which is entailed in today's decisions is for political not for judicial action. Until the Constitution is rewritten, we have the present one to support and construe.

The difficulty is, however, that this is precisely what each Justice thought and claimed to be doing—construing and supporting the Constitution. What Justice Douglas and the other dissenters meant was that the Court's precedents had settled and fixed the construction or interpretation of the Constitution, while the other Justices were not averse to a fresh look at the constitutional provisions, at least as far as concerned criminal procedure in State trials. One might say that ironically it was the "liberal" Justices, the "activists"—notably Justices Douglas, Brennan, and Marshall—who stood for *stare decisis* and the law of doctrines and concepts, while it was the "conservatives" and the "strict constructionists" who contended for a pragmatic, functional view of the Constitution, for allowing the States to have some room for "experimentation" when it came to administration of the criminal law. We see here what appears to be a reversal of roles, as those roles were perceived and attributed by journalists and the public opinion which they helped create or mold: the "activists" stood for non-action; the "strict constructionists" became "activists."

What these cases in the 1970s stand for with respect to the incorporation doctrine was correctly stated by Justice Brennan in his dissenting opinion, in which Justice Marshall joined:

> The majority of the Court remains of the view that, as in the case of every specific of the Bill of Rights that extends to the States, the Sixth Amendment's jury trial guarantee, however it is to be construed, has identical application against the State and Federal Governments.

This is a correct summary of the holdings insofar as the Sixth Amendment is construed as guaranteeing jury trial as an "interposition between the accused and his accuser of the commonsense judgment of a group of laymen." All other features do not go to the essence of the meaning of the term "jury" as the term is used in the Sixth Amendment as it is incorporated into the Fourteenth.

It would seem that this is essentially the *Palko* approach, although not denominated as such by the majority, for the Court is seeking to define that feature of the jury trial which makes it a fundamental right, and then every other aspect of such a trial takes on only an incidental quality, subject to acceptance, rejection or modification by the legislature.

The dissenting opinions by Justices Douglas, Brennan, Stewart, and Marshall all emphasized that the approval of the non-unanimous jury verdict creates the danger that the jury members from minority groups may be disregarded by the majority. The jurors' dissenting voices may not be considered or even heard. This may undermine public confidence in the jury system. As Justice Stewart wrote:

> For only a unanimous jury . . . can serve to minimize the potential bigotry of those who might convict on inadequate evidence, or acquit when evidence of guilt was clear. . . . The requirements of unanimity and impartial selection thus complement each other in ensuring the fair performance of the vital functions of a criminal court jury.

Justice White, in his plurality opinion in *Apodaca*, answered the argument about the suppression of a minority's views by pointing out that a defendant has no right to insist that a minority group be represented on his trial jury. The Constitution only forbids "systematic exclusion of identifiable segments of the community from jury panels and from juries ultimately drawn from those panels." No group, he said, has the right to block convictions. Furthermore, he said, the Court cannot assume that the majority of a jury will refuse to weigh the evidence or that it will disregard the minority's reasonable argument in favor of acquittal and act to convict on the basis of prejudice, or that it will disregard its instructions and cast its votes on the basis of prejudice rather than the evidence.

Justice Powell also considered the contention of the dissenting Justices regarding prejudice and bigotry by pointing out that the danger that a jury in a particular case will fail to meet its responsibility is inherent in any system that commits decisions of guilt or innocence to untrained laymen. Whether unanimity or majority-verdict is the rule, the jury system is premised on the conviction that each juror will faithfully perform his or her assigned duty.

Justice Powell also enumerated "protective devices" to diminish significantly the prospect of jury irresponsibility, such as peremptory challenges and challenges for cause when jurors are being selected; the judge's full jury instructions, with details concerning burden of proof, the duty of jurors to weigh the views of fellow jurors; the power of judges to set aside verdicts when the evidence is insufficient to convict; the power to direct acquittals when the evidence of guilt is lacking; the power to order a change of venue, and the power to impose restrictions on press coverage, in cases in which public emotion runs high or pretrial publicity prejudices a fair trial.

Justice Powell also referred to the fact that non-unanimous jury verdicts have been approved by the American Law Institute's Code of Criminal Procedure, by the British Parliament in the Criminal Justice Act of 1967, and by the Project on Standards for Criminal Justice of the American Bar Association.

IV.

We will recall that in *Hurtado*, in 1884, Justice Harlan argued for the single-rule doctrine, that is, that the Bill of Rights applies to the States in exactly the same way in which it applies to the Federal Government. His grandson, the second Justice Harlan, became the clearest, most explicit spokesman for the exactly opposite proposition. One may perhaps define the difference by saying that the first Justice Harlan was a nationalist, a Hamiltonian, when it came to the question of fundamental rights, while the second Justice Harlan was a federalist, a Jeffersonian. In the course of the years, the first Justice Harlan has proved to be the victor; in the 1970s it was clear that a majority of the Justices had adopted his position. But the second Justice Harlan has not been a voice crying in the wilderness. Justices Jackson and Fortas were clearly on his side, and in the 1970s it was apparent that Chief Justice Burger and Justices Powell and Rehnquist upheld his position—as a dissenting minority.

This division in the Court has been articulated almost definitively. In 1978, in *Ballew* v. *Georgia*,[21] the question was whether a trial for a misdemeanor before a jury of five persons, which was in accordance with a State statute, satisfied constitutional requirements. While the Court, for reasons not germane to our discussion, was unable to agree on an opinion, it did unanimously agree that a jury of five persons violated the defendant's constitutional rights. Four of the five opinions, however relied on *both* the Sixth and Fourteenth amendments, thus clearly implying that whatever the Sixth Amendment may require in a Federal case, the Fourteenth Amendment requires in a State case. This is made explicit in the concurring opinion of Justice Powell, with whom Chief Justice Burger and Justice Rehnquist agreed:

> I concur in the judgment [to reverse the conviction], as I agree that use of a jury as small as five members with authority to convict for serious offenses, involves grave questions of fairness. As the opinion of Mr. Justice Blackmun indicates, the line between five-and six-member juries is difficult to justify, but a line has to be drawn somewhere if the substance of jury trial is to be preserved.
>
> I do not agree, however, that every feature of jury trial practice must be the same in both federal and state courts. . . . Because the opinion of Mr. Justice Blackmun today assumes full incorporation of the Sixth Amendment by the Fourteenth Amendment, . . . I do not join it.

Once the Court rejected Justice Black's total incorporation doctrine, the Court should also have rejected the selective incorporation alternative, and instead have formulated a revised, refined version of the *Palko* doctrine, perhaps along the lines one finds in *Duncan* and in the opinions of the second Justice Harlan.

For one cannot logically select only some of the guarantees of the Bill of Rights for incorporation into the Fourteenth Amendment without resorting to some notion of fundamental rights. If, for example, the Seventh Amendment is held to be inapplicable to the States,[22] that can only be because the Court believes that the requirement of a jury trial in civil suits is not the guarantee of a fundamental right implicit in the concept of due process as this term is used in the Fourteenth Amendment.

The doctrine of selective incorporation, however, is by now too firmly established to be displaced, and so discretion may be taken to be the better part of logic. One may say with Justice Holmes that "upon this point a page of history is worth a volume of logic."[23] For if this century-old question were to be re-opened and re-argued, and its history were to be forgotten, there is the risk that old and established rights and liberties may be weakened or lost.[24] After a century of debate it may be best to act *as if* some of the guarantees of the first eight amendments have been selectively incorporated into the Due Process Clause, and apply equally to the Federal Government and the States.

We ought, however, to be aware of what is involved and of what we are, in reality, doing. It is of the utmost importance to believe and remember, as Justice Frankfurter pointed out, that "The Due Process Clause of the Fourteenth Amendment has an independent potency," that its meaning is not comprehended by the first eight amendments, nor is its meaning restricted to them,[25] and that, as Justice Harlan stressed, "The Bill of Rights is not necessarily irrelevant to the search for guidance in interpreting the Fourteenth Amendment, but the reason for and the nature of its relevance must be articulated,"[26] and that

> While the relevant inquiry may be aided by resort to one or more of the provisions of the Bill of Rights, it is not dependent on them or any of their radiations. The Due Process Clause of the Fourteenth Amendment stands, in my opinion, on its own bottom.[27]

Notes

1. *Hurtado* v. *California*, 110 U.S. 516 (1884).
2. *Beauharnais* v. *Illinois*, 343 U.S. 250 (1952).
3. *Roth* v. *United States*, 354 U.S. 470 (1957); Justice Harlan concurred in the State case, *Alberts* v. *California*, consolidated with *Roth*.
4. *Bloom* v. *Illinois*, 391 U.S. 194 (1968). Justice Fortas's concurring opinion should be read also as part of *Duncan* v. *Louisiana*, 391 U.S. 145 (1968), decided at the same time.
5. *Duncan* v. *Louisiana*, 391 U.S. 145 (1968).
6. For the statement by Justice Harlan, see his dissenting opinion, joined by Justice Stewart, in *Benton* v. *Maryland*, 395 U.S. 784 (1969), footnote 12; for statement by Justice Stewart, see his dissenting opinion in *Williams* v. *Florida*, 399 U.S. 78 (1970), opening paragraph; but cf. his dissenting opinion in *Apodaca* v. *Oregon*, 405, U.S. 404 (1972).
7. *Williams* v. Florida, 399 U.S. 78 (1970).
8. Cited in note 5 *supra*.
9. Cited in note 4 *supra*.
10. Italics in original.
11. *Palko* v. *Connecticut*, 302 U.S. 319 (1937).
12. Justice Harlan's opinion traced the process of selective incorporation in the Supreme Court beginning with *Mapp* v. *Ohio*, 367 U.S. 643 (1961).
13. The six-person jury was upheld as satisfying the Seventh Amendment's guarantee of trial by jury in civil cases in *Colegrove* v. *Battin*, 413 U.S. 149 (1973).
14. *Benton* v. *Maryland*, 395 U.S. 784 (1969).
15. *Apodaca* v. *Oregon*, 406 U.S. 404 (1972).
16. *Adamson* v. *California*, 332 U.S. 46 (1947), dissenting opinion of Justice Black.
17. For example, *Duncan* v. *Louisiana*, 391 U.S. 145 (1968).
18. The court added that the reasonable-doubt rule is rooted in due process and was rejected in *Johnson* v. *Louisiana*, 406 U.S. 356 (1972), decided on the same day as *Apodaca* case.
19. The concurring and dissenting opinions appear in *Johnson* v. *Louisiana*, cited in

note 18 supra, except for the brief dissenting opinion of Justice Stewart, with Justices Brennan and Marshall joining, which appears in *Apodaca*.

20. Justice Douglas reviewed all the precedents, starting with *Gitlow* v. *N. Y.*, 268 U.S. 652 (1925), through *Mapp* v. *Ohio*, 367 U.S. 643 (1961).
21. *Ballew* v. *Ga.*, 435 U.S. 223 (1978).
22. *Colegrove* v. *Battin*, 413 U.S.149 (1973), dissenting opinion of Justice Marshall at p. 169, footnote 4.
23. *New York Trust Co.* v. *Eisner*, 256 U.S. 345 (1921).
24. Cf. *Screws* v. *U.S.*, 325 U.S. 91 (1945), opinion of Justice Rutledge at p. 120.
25. *Adamson* v. *Calif.*, 332 U.S. 46 (1947), concurring opinion of Justice Frankfurter.
26. *Duncan* v. *Louisiana*, 391 U.S. 145 (1968), dissenting opinion of Justice Harlan.
27. *Griswold* v. *Conn.*, 381 U.S. 479 (1965), concurring opinion of Justice Harlan.

6

"Liberty" Beyond the
Bill of Rights

I.

In *Corfield*,[1] decided only thirty-two years after the Bill of Rights went into effect, Justice Washington, when considering what the words "privileges" and "immunities" meant, spoke of rights "which are in their very nature, fundamental, which belong, of right, to the citizens of all free governments." *He did not say that "privileges" and "immunities" could be defined only by the rights guaranteed by the Bill of Rights.*

After the adoption of the Fourteenth Amendment, as we have seen, there were dissenting members of the Court—most notably Justices Field and Bradley—who maintained that the amendment referred to "the natural and inalienable rights which belong to all citizens." They went beyond the Bill of Rights to the Declaration of Independence, which, they contended, was the basis for the rights intended to be protected by the amendment, "rights which are the gift of the Creator; which the law does not confer, but only recognizes."[2]

The first Justice Harlan likewise was willing to look beyond the confines of the first eight amendments for "the fundamental rights of life, liberty, [and] property." These fundamental rights, he asserted, are only "principally" enumerated in the Bill of Rights.[3] He held that the Fourteenth Amendment guarantees rights the abridgment of which "shocks or ought to shock the sense of right and justice [of] everyone who loves liberty."[4]

It was this line of thought which, as we have seen, culminated, in 1923, in the decision of the Court in *Meyer* v. *Nebraska*,[5] stating that the "liberty" protected by the Due Process Clause of the Fourteenth Amendment embraces the right to acquire useful knowledge; and two years later, in *Pierce* v. *Society of Sisters*,[6] the Court declared a State statute unconstitutional as an interference with the liberty of parents to direct the upbringing and education of their children. These decisions did not incorporate any of the first eight amendments into the Fourteenth Amendment. They gave substantive content to the term "liberty" as the term is used in the Due Process Clause. These decisions gave solid constitutional respectability and sanction to *the principle that the Bill of Rights is by no means the exclusive source of constitutional rights and liberties; that the term "liberty" as used in the Fourteenth Amendment comprehends all fundamental rights.*

Although *Palko* v. *Connecticut*[7] involved procedural due process, the basic thrust of Justice Cardozo's opinion was broad enough to comprehend substantive due process as well, for the opinion spoke of values that are "of the very essence of a scheme of ordered liberty," of a "principle of justice so rooted in the traditions and conscience of our people as to be ranked as fundamental," of a State law imposing "a hardship so acute and shocking that our polity will not endure it," and of "fundamental principles of liberty and justice, which lie at the base of all our civil and political institutions." While the Supreme Court thirty-two years later[8] expressly overruled *Palko*, its decision had no effect on cases that involved the question of fundamental rights that are not among those enumerated in the Bill of Rights and are, therefore, beyond the reach of the rule of selective incorporation.

An analysis of several cases will illustrate the process by which the term "liberty" has been used by the Court to establish, constitutionally, fundamental rights which have an existence not rooted in the specific enumeration of the first eight amendments.

II.

In their dissenting opinions in the *Slaughter-House Cases*,[9] Justices Field and Bradley spoke of liberty of contract; about a quarter of a century later liberty of contract became part of American constitutional law, and the idea of substantive liberty or substantive due process became accepted constitutional doctrine. The Court in *Allgeyer* v. *Louisiana*,[10] decided in 1897, made this significant statement:

> The liberty mentioned in that [Fourteenth] Amendment means not only the right of the citizen to be free from the mere physical restraint of his person, as by incarceration, but the term is deemed to embrace the right of the citizen to be free in the enjoyment of all his faculties; to be free to use them in all lawful ways; to live and work where he will; to earn his livelihood by any lawful calling; to pursue any livelihood or avocation, and for that purpose to enter into all contracts which may be proper, necessary, and essential to his carrying out to a successful conclusion the purposes above mentioned.

The substance and spirit of this statement, despite the great social, economic and political changes which have taken place in the twentieth century, still have force. But at this point we shall concentrate on the liberty of contract, which is the culmination of the rights or liberties enumerated in the above quotation and which has generally become identified with the case of *Lochner* v. *New York*,[11] decided in 1905.

In *Lochner*, the Court, by 5–4 vote, held that a law restricting employment in bakeries to ten hours per day and sixty hours per week was an unconstitutional abridgment of the right of adult workers to make contracts with respect to their means of making a living. Although considerable medical evidence had been introduced in support of the New York law, the Court by-passed this evidence and said that while the work of a baker may not be as healthy as some other types of work, it is vastly more healthy than many other kinds. "It might be safely affirmed that almost all occupations more or less affect health. . . . But are we all, on that account, at the mercy of legislative majorities?"

Justice Harlan, dissenting, stressed the weight of the medical evidence exposing the dangers in the type of work involved, and that it was the responsibility of the legislature, and not of the courts, to consider and weigh that evidence, and that legislative enactments should be enforced by the courts "unless they are plainly and palpably, beyond all question, in violation of the fundamental law of the Constitution."

The dissenting opinion of Justice Holmes is one of the most famous of American judicial opinions. The case, he said, was decided

> upon an economic theory which a large part of the country does not entertain. . . . The Fourteenth Amendment does not enact Mr. Herbert Spencer's *Social Statics*. . . . I

think that the word liberty, in the Fourteenth Amendment, is perverted when it is held to prevent the natural outcome of a dominant opinion, unless it can be said that a rational and fair man necessarily would admit that the statute proposed would infringe *fundamental principles as they have been understood by the traditions of our people and our law.*

While the *Lochner* approach, with its emphasis on liberty of contract, was not consistently followed by the Court, it was, however, the dominant philosophy and came to characterize the Court until discredited by the Court's majority in 1937. It has been estimated that between 1899 and 1937 the Court had invalidated State or Federal regulations in 197 cases.[12] In 1937 the Court began to uphold the constitutionality of congressional New Deal legislation which substantially interfered with, and in some instances wholly annulled, liberty of contract.[13] In 1949 the Court explicitly abrogated the *Lochner* doctrine.[14]

But it should be emphasized that the repudiation of the *Lochner* doctrine meant, to the Court's majority, only that there would be thereafter little likelihood of judicial interference with legislative regulation of the economic sphere; repudiation of *Lochner* meant that the Court would uphold legislation regulating economic activities if there are any facts that would support the reasonableness of the legislative judgment. The end of *Lochner* did not mean, however, the end of substantive liberty or substantive due process. The term "liberty" in the Due Process Clause was not erased from the Constitution; it was still there, and continued, as it were, to ask for interpretation and application. Liberty of contract became a curious, if not scandalous, fact of constitutional history; but the concept of liberty, freed from economic associations, retained life and even, in time, gained vigor and honor. The reasoning of *Allgeyer* and of *Lochner* with respect to the generating force of "liberty" guaranteed by the Constitution has been fully endorsed. The decisions of these cases have been discredited, but much of the opinions is fully viable.

III.

For our purposes, perhaps the best introduction to the enhanced force given to the concept of liberty—and to the subject of substantive liberty or substantive due process—will be a discussion of *Griswold* v. *Connecticut*,[15] decided by the Court in 1965.

A Connecticut statute declared use of contraceptives a criminal offense. The executive and medical directors of the Planned Parenthood League were convicted on a charge of having violated the statute as accessories by giving information, instruction and advice to married persons as to the means of preventing conception. The Supreme Court, by 7–2 vote, reversed the convictions.

In his opinion for the Court, Justice Douglas noted that "Overtones of some arguments suggest that *Lochner* v. *New York* should be our guide. But we decline that invitation. . . . " In order to separate the instant case from *Lochner*, clearly and emphatically, Justice Douglas wrote, with an eye on *Lochner*:

> We do not sit as a super-legislature to determine the wisdom, need, and propriety of laws that touch economic problems, business affairs; or social conditions. This [Connecticut] law, however, operates directly on an intimate relation of husband and wife. . . .

Then Justice Douglas referred to rights which, though not mentioned in the Bill of Rights, have been recognized by the Court: freedom of association, the right of parents to educate their child in a school of their choice (public, private or parochial), and the right to study any particular subject or any foreign language. Re-interpreting the *Pierce*[16] and *Meyer*[17] cases, Justice Douglas said that the Court had in these cases construed the First Amendment to include certain of these rights and were made applicable to the States by force of the Fourteenth Amendment. So, too, the right of freedom of speech includes the right to distribute, the right to receive, the right to read, freedom of inquiry, freedom of thought, freedom to teach, "indeed the freedom of the entire university community. . . . Without those peripheral rights the specific rights [of the First Amendment] would be less secure. And so we reaffirm the principle of *Pierce* and the *Meyer* cases." So, too, freedom of association is "a peripheral First Amendment right."[18] From these instances Justice Douglas moved to a general statement:

> . . . specific guarantees in the Bill of Rights have penumbras, formed by emanations from these guarantees that help give them life and substance. . . . Various guarantees create zones of privacy.

What specific guarantees of the Bill of Rights create "zones of privacy" as their "penumbras"? The Court's opinion enumerated the following: the right of association, the Third Amendment prohibition against the quartering of soldiers in any house in time of peace without the consent of the owner, the Fourth Amendment right of persons to be secure "in their persons, houses, papers, and effects, against unreasonable searches and seizures," and the Fifth Amendment in its guarantee against self-incrimination. The opinion also added at this point the Ninth Amendment: "The enumeration in the Constitution, of certain rights, shall not be construed to deny or disparage others retained by the people." Justice Douglas concluded that the instant case, then, "concerns a relationship lying within the zone of privacy created by several fundamental constitutional guarantees." "We deal," he said,

> with a right of privacy older than the Bill of Rights—older than our political parties, older than our school system. . . . [Marriage] is an association that promotes a way of life, not causes; a harmony in living, not political faiths; a bilateral loyalty, not commercial or social projects. Yet it is an association for as noble a purpose as any involved in our prior decisions.

Justice Douglas's opinion is consistent with the incorporation doctrine, but a doctrine now stretched to incorporate into the Fourteenth Amendment the "penumbras, formed by emanations" from the guarantees explicitly formulated in the Bill of Rights. The implication may be that the fundamental rights of Americans are only those enumerated in the Constitution—rights, however, that are liberally interpreted.

Justice Goldberg's concurring opinion, in which Chief Justice Warren and Justice Brennan joined, took, however, the fundamental rights line. At the outset Justice Goldberg stated that, although he does not accept the view that the Due Process Clause incorporates all of the first eight amendments,

> I do agree *that the concept of liberty protects those personal rights that are fundamental, and is not confined to the specific terms of the Bill of Rights.* (Italics supplied.)

In a footnote, Justice Goldberg noted that the Court "has never held that the Bill of Rights or the Fourteenth Amendment protects only those rights that the Constitution specifically mentions by name." The opinion emphatically formulates a fundamental rights doctrine. It quotes Justice Cardozo for the proposition that the Due Process Clause protects those liberties that are "so rooted in the traditions and conscience of our people as to be ranked as fundamental,"[19] and from the *Gitlow*[20] opinion that freedom of speech and of the press "are among the *fundamental* personal rights and 'liberties' protected by the due process clause. . . . " (italics added by Justice Goldberg). The following passage effectively summarizes his position:

> This Court, in a series of decisions, has held that the Fourteenth Amendment absorbs and applies to the States those specifics of the first eight amendments which express fundamental personal rights. The language and history of the Ninth Amendment reveal that the Framers of the Constitution believed that there are additional fundamental rights, protected from governmental infringement, which exist alongside those fundamental rights specifically mentioned in the first eight constitutional amendments.

Although Justice Goldberg's opinion treats elaborately of the history and wording of the Ninth Amendment, it is clear that its basic premise is that the guarantee of "liberty" is a guarantee of *fundamental rights*—a guarantee of substantive liberty, as well as of procedural liberty or procedural due process. The Ninth Amendment, said Justice Goldberg,

> shows a belief of the Constitution's authors that fundamental rights exist that are not expressly enumerated in the first eight amendments and an intent that the list of rights included there not be deemed exhaustive. . . . The Ninth Amendment simply shows the intent of the Constitution's authors that other fundamental personal rights should not be denied such protection or disparaged in any other way simply because they are not specifically listed in the first eight amendments. I do not see how this broadens the authority of the Court; rather it seems to support what this Court has been doing in protecting fundamental rights.

The entire opinion is, indeed, replete with phrases that reiterate the theme of fundamental rights—e.g., "fundamental liberties of citizens," "fundamental personal rights," "fundamental personal liberties," "fundamental rights"—and that regardless whether such fundamental rights are or are not explicitly mentioned in the Constitution, they are included in the "liberty" which the Fourteenth Amendment guarantees against abridgment by any State.

The logic of the argument from the Ninth Amendment is not altogether clear, since it was well established that the first ten amendments originally had been intended as limitations only on the Federal Government.[21] What Justice Goldberg meant, then, was that just as the term "liberty" in the Fourteenth Amendment has absorbed the fundamental rights guaranteed by some of the first eight amendments, so, too, has it absorbed the Ninth Amendment, i.e., all other fundamental rights, even if not explicitly enumerated in the Bill of Rights.

Justice Harlan, in a concurring opinion, stated that just as he objected to Justice Black's incorporation doctrine, which *imposed*, without differentiation, all of the provisions of the Bill of Rights on the States, so, too, did he object to Justice Douglas's reformulation, which appears to broaden the terms of the Bill of Rights by including their "penumbras," but in fact *restricts* the reach of the Due Process Clause of the Bill of Rights to "the letter and the penumbra of the Bill of Rights." He would hold the Connecticut statute unconstitutional, he wrote, because "the enactment violates basic values 'implicit in the concept of ordered liberty,' *Palko* v. *Connecticut*." While the relevant inquiry, he said, may be aided by resort to provisions of the Bill of Rights, "it is not dependent on them or any of their radiations. *The Due Process Clause of the Fourteenth Amendment stands, in my opinion, on its own bottom*." (Italics supplied.)

Thus, Justice Harlan would have looked only on the generating power of the concept of "liberty" in the Due Process Clause. But how will one fill the "vague contours of the Due Process Clause" without "introducing their own notions of constitutional right and wrong"? But, Justice Harlan argued, the incorporation process does not really solve this problem, for the specific terms of the amendments that comprise the Bill of Rights lend themselves just as readily as does the Due Process Clause to "personal" interpretations. Judicial self-restraint can be achieved in the constitutional area, he said,

> only by continual insistence upon respect for the teachings of history, solid recognition of the basic values that underlie our society, and wise appreciation of the great roles that the doctrines of federalism and separation of powers played in establishing and preserving American freedoms. . . . Adherence to these principles will not, of course, obviate all constitutional differences of opinion among judges, nor should it. Their continued recognition will, however, go farther towards keeping most judges from roaming at large in the constitutional field than will the interpolation into the Constitution of an artificial and largely illusory restriction on the content of the Due Process Clause [by merely incorporating into the Clause the Bill of Rights].

In a footnote at this point, Justice Harlan noted that Justice Black, in arguing for the incorporation doctrine, was "forced to lay aside a host of cases in which the Court has recognized fundamental rights in the Fourteenth Amendment *without specific reliance upon the Bill of Rights*." (Italics supplied.)

In a concurring opinion, Justice White declared that the Connecticut law deprived married couples of "liberty" without due process of law.

Citing *Meyer* and *Pierce*, Justice White stated that there is a realm of family life which the State may not enter "without substantial justification," which was absent from the instant case. The opinion made no reference to any provision of the Constitution other than the Due Process Clause of the Fourteenth Amendment.

Justice Black, with Justice Stewart joining, dissented. He said that he could find nothing in the Constitution about a "right of privacy." He found no substance in the talk about a constitutional right of privacy "as an emanation from one or more constitutional provisions." He contended that the position of Justices Harlan and White is based on "natural justice" or other formulas "which mean the same thing," and in a footnote listed phrases from earlier decisions under which laws were struck down under the Fourteenth Amendment:

"shocks the conscience"
"decencies of civilized conduct"
"some principle of justice so rooted in the traditions and conscience of our people as to be ranked as fundamental"
"those canons of decency and fairness which express the notions of justice of English-speaking peoples"
"the community's sense of fair play"
"deeply rooted feelings of the community"
"fundamental notions of fairness and justice"
"rights . . . basic to our free society"
"fundamental principles of liberty and justice"
"denial of fundamental fairness, shocking to the natural sense of justice."

All such formulas require judges to strike down laws as unconstitutional "on the basis of their own appraisal of what laws are unwise or unnecessary." The power to make such decisions, however, is a legislative one. "I do not believe that we are granted power . . . to measure constitutionality by our belief that legislation . . . is offensive to our own notions of 'civilized standards of conduct.'" The Court in the instant case, said Justice Black, in fact adhered to the discredited *Lochner* doctrine, which was also reflected in the *Meyer* and *Pierce* cases, "the same natural law due process philosophy which many later opinions repudiated, and which I cannot accept." How, Justice Black asked, is the Court to determine that a State law indeed violates "fundamental principles of liberty and justice" or that it is contrary to the "traditions and [collective] conscience of our people"? Is the Court to use and rely on a Gallup Poll? Will there be a scientific device by which the Court could determine what traditions are rooted in the "[collective] conscience of our people"? The Court has no constitutional power, based on the Ninth Amendment "or any mysterious and uncertain natural law concept" for striking down the Connecticut law. The *Lochner* doctrine, based on subjective considerations of "natural justice," "is no less dangerous when used to enforce this Court's views about personal rights than those about economic rights."

Justice Stewart, in a separate dissenting opinion in which Justice Black joined, stated that he could find no provision anywhere in the Bill of Rights or in any other part of the Constitution that guarantees a right of privacy.

Summarizing the various opinions in *Griswold*, we find the following propositions relevant to our concern with the idea of fundamental rights:

1. The opinion of Justice Douglas for the Court broadens the specific, explicit guarantees of the Bill of Rights by taking into account the "penumbras," formed by "emanations" from the specific provisions. In arriving at the conclusion that there is a constitutional right of privacy, Justice Douglas referred to six amendments—First, Third, Fourth, Fifth, Ninth, and Fourteenth. The right of privacy is an "emanation" from the specific guarantees of the Bill of Rights, which are incorporated into the "liberty" of the Due Process Clause of the Fourteenth Amendment.

2. Justice Goldberg took the position that the concept of "liberty" protects all rights that are fundamental—those which are specifically enumerated in the Bill of Rights and those which are not. The purpose of the Ninth Amendment is precisely to protect those fundamental rights which were not spelled out in the first eight amendments.

> . . . the Ninth Amendment shows a belief of the Constitution's authors that fundamental rights exist that are not expressly enumerated in the first eight amendments and an intent that the list of rights included there not be deemed exhaustive.

3. Justice Harlan contended that Justice Douglas's concentration on the guarantees of the Bill of Rights exclusively *restricts* the liberty guaranteed by the Fourteenth Amendment against the States. The liberty guaranteed by that amendment is intended to condemn any enactment that violates basic values "implicit in the concept of ordered liberty."[22] Justice White on the whole shared this view.

4. Justice Black (with Justice Stewart joining) found no right of

privacy among the enumerated guarantees, no broad guarantee of fundamental rights in the Constitution, no warrant for any "natural law due process philosophy," no basis in the Constitution for substantive due process.

These opinions give a fair reflection of the positions of the Court on the meaning of fundamental rights and their constitutional roots and reach. (The Court when it decided *Griswold* was comprised of Chief Justice Warren, and Justices Black, Douglas, Clark, Harlan, Brennan, Stewart, White and Goldberg.)

IV.

A case on substantive liberty, or substantive due process, that may be taken as representative of the approaches of the Burger Court is *Moore* v. *City of East Cleveland*,[23] decided in 1977, in which five new members of the post-Warren era participated; namely, Chief Justice Burger and Justices Blackmun, Powell, Rehnquist, and Stevens, the first four appointed by President Nixon, Justice Stevens by President Ford.

A housing ordinance of East Cleveland, Ohio, in limiting occupancy of a dwelling unit to members of a single family, defined "family" as essentially the nuclear family of parents and their children. Mrs. Moore lived in her home with her son and two grandsons. The grandsons, however, were not brothers but first cousins. She was convicted by the State courts of violating the ordinance. The conviction was reversed by 5–4 vote. Justice Powell announced the judgment of the Court in which only three Justices joined—Brennan, Marshall, and Blackmun. There were two concurring and three dissenting opinions, six opinions in all. The dissenters were Chief Justice Burger and Justices Stewart, Rehnquist, and White.

Justice Powell, citing *Meyer* and *Pierce*, said that there is a private realm of family life which the State may not enter. The City of East Cleveland, while willing to grant this proposition, contended, however, that these cases gave grandmothers no "fundamental rights with respect to grandsons," and that constitutional family rights extended only to the nuclear family. Justice Powell countered this position by contending that the basic reasons underlying the decisions in which parental authority was upheld extend to the facts in the instant case; for the underlying reasons in *Meyer*, *Pierce*, and related cases are history and tradition, which give content to the substantive meaning of "liberty." History and tradition support a larger conception of family than that which constitutes the nuclear family.

> Our decisions establish that the Constitution protects the sanctity of the family precisely because the institution of the family is deeply rooted in this nation's history and tradition. It is through the family that we inculcate and pass down many of our most cherished values, moral and cultural.
>
> Ours is by no means a tradition limited to respect for the bonds uniting the members of the nuclear family. The tradition of uncles, aunts, cousins, and especially, grandparents sharing a household along with parents and children has roots equally venerable and equally deserving of constitutional recognition.

In a notable footnote Justice Powell rejected the argument that reliance on history and tradition will broaden the reach of the Due Process Clause. On the contrary, he said, "an approach grounded in history imposes limits on the judiciary that are more meaningful than any based on the abstract formula taken from *Palko*. . . . "

Justice Powell quoted with emphatic approval the following passage from an opinion of Justice Harlan[24] on the process by which content is given to the Due Process Clause:

> Due process has not been reduced to any formula; its content cannot be determined by reference to any code. The best that can be said is that through the course of this Court's decisions it has represented the balance which our Nation, built upon postulates of respect for the liberty of the individual, has struck between that liberty and the demands of organized society. If the supply of content to this Constitutional concept has of necessity been a rational process, it certainly has not been one where judges have felt free to roam where unguided speculation might take them. The balance of which I speak is the balance struck by this country, *having regard to what history teaches are the traditions from which it developed as well as the traditions from which it broke.* That tradition is a *living thing*. . . .
>
> [T]he full scope of the liberty guaranteed by the Due Process Clause cannot be found in or limited by the precise terms of the specific guarantees elsewhere provided in the Constitution. . . .

The plurality opinion recognized explicitly the "treacherous field" that substantive due process offers, as demonstrated by the *Lochner* era. "That history counsels caution and restraint. But it does not counsel abandonment. . . . " It certainly does not counsel the Court to draw arbitrary lines, but rather "'respect for the teachings of history [and] solid recognition of the basic values that underlie our society.'"

This opinion by Justice Powell is clearly consonant with the fundamental rights approach of Justices Cardozo, Frankfurter, and Harlan, notably formulated in *Palko*, except for Justice White's emendation in footnote 14 in his opinion for the Court in *Duncan* v. *Louisiana*.[25] It should be noted that the plurality opinion in *Moore* was for two Justices (Brennan and Marshall) who belonged to the Warren Court and two (Powell and Blackmun) who had been appointed by President Nixon.

Justice Brennan's concurring opinion, in which Justice Marshall joined, wholly approved the plurality opinion but only underscored the arbitrary character of the definition of "family" in the East Cleveland ordinance "in the light of the tradition of the American home that has been a feature of our society since our beginning as a Nation—the 'tradition' in the plurality's words, 'of uncles, aunts, cousins, and especially grandparents sharing a household along with parents and children. . . .'"

Justice Stevens's concurring opinion took another track altogether. His objection to the ordinance was that it unconstitutionally abridged "a fundamental right normally associated with the ownership of residential property."

Chief Justice Burger, dissenting, avoided the constitutional issue and would have decided against Mrs. Moore for her failure to exhaust administrative remedies to seek a variance from the zoning ordinance.

Justice Stewart's dissenting opinion, in which Justice Rehnquist joined, focused, like the plurality opinion, on the fundamental rights issue, only it came out at the opposite end. Mrs. Moore's claim conceivably could be tied to the contention that the ordinance abridged her fundamental right of association or her fundamental right of privacy. Her ties of kinship, however, Justice Stewart concluded, cannot be elevated to associational freedom or the right of privacy.

Freedom of association, he said, has been recognized because it is often indispensable to the effectuation of explicit First Amendment guarantees: "the promotion of speech, assembly, press, or religion." While "the outer boundaries of constitutional protection of freedom of association" may not be known, "they surely do not extend to those who assert no interest other than the gratification, convenience, and economy of sharing the same residence." The "biological fact of common ancestry" does not necessarily give "related persons" constitutional rights of association. The interest that Mrs. Moore has in sharing her home with her grandsons simply does not rise to the level of those personal interests which have been deemed "'implicit in the concept of ordered liberty'. . . . See *Roe* v. *Wade*,[26] quoting *Palko* v. *Connecticut.*" These personal interests, centering upon "private family life," which are constitutionally protected include a woman's right to decide whether to terminate pregnancy, freedom to marry a person of another race, the right to use contraceptives, parents' right to send children to private schools, and parents' right to have children instructed in a foreign language. The opinion strongly intimates that the right of parents living with their unemancipated children would also be included among the personal interests that should be constitutionally protected.

Justice White's dissenting opinion accepts the idea that constitutional adjudication includes the right of the Court to protect substantive due process, but this power should be used only when necessary to protect "'all fundamental rights comprised within the term liberty.'"[27] It is not enough that the Court finds legislation to be "merely arbitrary or unreasonable." If the legislation does not abridge a fundamental right, the Court "should be extremely reluctant to breathe still further substantive content into the Due Process Clause so as to strike down legislation adopted by a State or city to promote its welfare." The threshold question is whether the challenged legislation is a deprivation of "liberty." *Meyer, Palko* and more recent cases assert that "only fundamental liberties will be given *substantive* protection. . . ."[28] Justice White did not think that Mrs. Moore's claim could be identified as a fundamental right.

> To say that one has a personal right to live with all . . . of one's grandchildren and that this right is implicit in ordered liberty [*Palko*] is, as my Brother Stewart says, "to extend the limited substantive contours of the Due Process Clause beyond recognition." The present claim is hardly one of which it could be said that "neither liberty nor justice would exist if [it] were sacrificed." *Palko* v. *Connecticut.*

Justice White questioned resort to tradition for the determination of what to include in the concept of substantive due process, in the concept of fundamental rights.

> What the deeply rooted traditions of the country are is arguable; which of them deserve the protection of the Due Process Clause is even more debatable.

An overview of the case shows that Mrs. Moore's claim was upheld by two of the Warren Court Justices (Brennan and Marshall) and three of the Nixon-Ford appointees, Justices Powell, Blackmun, and Stevens, and that of the four dissenters, two—Justices Stewart and White—were members of the Warren Court, and two—Chief Justice Burger and Justice Rehnquist—had been appointed by President Nixon. The Burger Court by no means scrapped the idea of substantive liberty or substantive due process. In a case decided in 1976, the Court,[29] in an opinion by Justice Rehnquist, said that the Due Process Clause "affords not only a procedural guarantee against the deprivation of 'liberty,' but likewise protects substantive aspects of liberty against unconstitutional restrictions by the State." There could hardly be a clearer positive statement upholding the concept of substantive due process following the emphatic discrediting of the *Lochner* era.

There are differences of opinion on the important question how the Court can tell what claims or interests to consider as coming within the guarantee of substantive liberty encompassed by the Due Process Clause. Justices Stewart and Rehnquist held substantially to the *Palko* approach with its stress on the concept of "ordered liberty"; Justices Powell, Brennan, Marshall, and Blackmun spoke of the sanctity of the family as deeply rooted in American history and tradition; Justice White questioned the usefulness of resort to tradition—there is argument as to what the traditions are, and more important, there remains the more difficult and meaningful problem of choosing what traditions to give protection under the Due Process Clause.

But this debate was not peculiar to the Burger Court. It went on, as we saw, in the Warren Court, in which Justice Black rejected altogether the notion of fundamental rights and held to the total incorporation doctrine, while Justice Harlan was spokesman for the exact opposite position—rejection of the incorporation doctrine and avowal of the fundamental rights idea, with heavy leaning on the *Palko* approach.

In the Burger Court the lines may not have been so tautly drawn. It was harder to foretell how most of the Justices would vote and why. Perhaps there was more pragmatism and less doctrine. The term "liberty" lends itself to many approaches and many meanings. It ought not to be defined with exactness, and the future history of the Court will show as much diversity of views as is shown by its past history.

In a case decided in 1976,[30] involving the transfer of inmates from a medium security prison to a maximum security institution, without adequate fact-finding hearings, the majority opinion upholding the transfer was by Justice White, a member of the Warren Court, while the dissenters were Justice Stevens, a Ford appointee, and Justices Brennan and Marshall; but more than the division, it is significant that it was Justice Stevens who wrote the following statement in his dissenting opinion—a statement that has in it strong echoes from Justices Washington, Field, Bradley, the first Harlan, and McReynolds of the *Meyer* and *Pierce* opinions:

> [It is not true that the Constitution and State laws are the only sources of a "liberty interest."]
>
> If a man were the creature of the State, the analysis would be correct. But neither the Bill of Rights nor the laws of sovereign States create the liberty which the Due Process Clause protects. The relevant constitutional provisions are limitations on the power of the sovereign to infringe on the liberty of the citizen. The relevant state laws either create property rights, or they curtail the freedom of the citizen who must live in an ordered society. Of course, law is essential to the exercise and enjoyment of individual liberty in a complex society. But it is not the source of liberty, and surely not the exclusive source.
>
> I had thought it self-evident that all men were endowed by their Creator with liberty as one of the cardinal unalienable rights. It is that basic freedom which the Due Process Clause protects, rather than the particular rights or privileges conferred by specific laws or regulations.

This statement, with its explicit terms and overtones, goes back of the Constitution to the Declaration of Independence, the theories of John Locke, and the Stoic teachings of Natural Law—which filtered into *Palko*, and against which Justice Black, a leading "liberal" on the Warren Court, vehemently protested time and again.

After hearing the discordant voices of the Justices of the Supreme Court, it can nonetheless be said that the principle of fundamental rights has been firmly fixed as a significant part of the Constitution. The reasons for adherence to the principle vary from Justice to Justice, but there is no warrant for fear that the principle itself is threatened. In the mid-1930s four Justices who consistently opposed New Deal economic and social legislation came to be known as the Four Horsemen of the Apocalypse. Now there are only two who hear a different drumbeat than that which the others hear. Unlike the Four Horsemen, Justices Scalia and Thomas would not oppose legislation; on the contrary, they would use the mere reasonableness test, not the strict scrutiny test, to uphold the constitutionality of laws and State actions that the other Justices would find to be infringements of fundamental rights. It is not likely that they will win converts to their idiosyncratic opinion. Indeed, to a limited extent Justice Scalia has himself made an important concession, if not to the principle of fundamental rights, at least to the doctrine of incorporation; for, in a case decided in January 1994, in a brief concurring opinion, he wrote:

> Except insofar as our decisions have included within the Fourteenth Amendment certain explicit substantive protections of the Bill of Rights—an extension I accept because it is both long established and narrowly limited—I reject the proposition that the Due Process Clause guarantees certain (unspecified) liberties,[31] . . .

Later in the same year, 1994, Justices Scalia and Thomas joined in an opinion for the Court by Chief Justice Rehnquist that can hardly be said to have "narrowly limited" the substantive protections of the Bill of Rights—indeed, that opened up the meaning of the Bill of Rights. Although the case—as often happens—is hardly important on the facts, it is quite important jurisprudentially. The case of *Dolan* v. *City of Tigard*[32] involved the Takings Clause of the Fifth Amendment, that provides "[N]or shall private property be taken for public use, without just compensation." The Court was asked to decide whether the requirement by a city that certain land be dedicated to the city as a condition imposed on the city's approval of the lot owner's building permit constitutes an uncompensated taking in violation of the Constitution. By a 5–4 decision, the Court held: (1) "The Takings Clause of the Fifth Amendment of the United States Constitution, [has been] made applicable to the States through the Fourteenth Amendment . . . " (2) The "reasonable relationship" test is not applicable, nor is the "exacting scrutiny" test applicable. What is applicable is an intermediate test, which a dissenting opinion correctly characterized as a test of "heightened scrutiny." In other words, neither the minimal nor the maximum scrutiny is to be used in such a case, but an in-between measure of scrutiny. Although the case involved a property/business claim, in which, since 1937, only the minimum scrutiny test has been applied, Chief Justice Rehnquist wrote (with echoes of Justice Frankfurter's words in the Second Flag Salute Case): "We see no reason why the Takings Clause of the Fifth Amendment, as much a part of the Bill of Rights as the First Amendment or Fourteenth Amendment, should be relegated to the status of a poor relation. . . . " (3) The burden of proof rests on the State—a burden that the State had not met.

In a dissenting opinion by Justice Stevens (joined by Justices Blackmun and Ginsburg; Justice Souter dissented in a separate opinion), it was argued that the Court has resurrected "a species of substantive due process analysis that it firmly rejected decades ago." Justice Stevens associated the majority approach with a case that "applied the same kind of substantive due process analysis more frequently identified with a better known case that accorded similar substantive protection to a baker's *liberty interest* in working 60 hours a week and 10 hours a day. See *Lochner* v. *New York*." (Italics supplied.) In other words, according to the dissenting opinion, the majority did not share Justice Black's opinion that the Fourteenth Amendment was intended to "incorporate" all of the provisions of the Bill of Rights, including the Takings Clause, but instead looked to the "liberty" guaranteed by the Due Process Clause and held that it generated or encompassed the Takings Clause guarantee. If this is the case, then the Court placed the mantle of substantive due process on the Takings Clause. Since the repudiation of *Lochner*, a State's action affecting an economic interest is presumed to be constitutional, and the test of its constitutionality when challenged is one of "reasonableness," and the burden of proof is not on the State but on the litigant who contests the action.

Thus, according to the three dissenting Justices, the majority opinion has departed from well-established precedents in a number of respects: (1) It has subjected an action of the State in the economic sphere, not to the test of reasonableness (which was the test that should have been used), nor to the strict scrutiny test applicable where a fundamental right is infringed, but to a newly devised intermediate or "heightened" scrutiny test. (2) It created a new substantive due process constitutional right.

Overarching the great differences between the majority and the three dissenting Justices, there is the statement by Chief Justice Rehnquist, and agreed to by the two staunch conservatives, Justices Scalia and Thomas, that a guarantee of the Fifth Amendment, which is a limit on the Federal Government, "is applicable to the States through the Fourteenth Amendment." No matter what theory is subscribed to by these Justices (the opinion is bare of theoretical propositions), they in fact affirm that the guarantees of the Bill of Rights have been selectively incorporated into the Fourteenth Amendment. There, therefore, need be no concern that this development—the most important development in American constitutional law in the twentieth century—is in danger of being undone.

V.

One would think that a decision of the Supreme Court declaring, for the first time, that women have a fundamental constitutional right to terminate a pregnancy would be almost universally hailed and welcomed as still another gain for liberty, that American society would give the decision three hearty cheers. But, as we know, this did not happen. Instead, *Roe* v. *Wade*, decided in 1973, has generated more heated controversy, has caused wider and deeper political and religious divisions, than has any other Supreme Court decision in the twentieth century. The school desegregation case, *Brown* v. *Board of Education*[33] (1954), caused much agitation, some States and municipalities fiercely resisted judicial orders to desegregate their school systems, but a relatively short time later saw a subsidence of the revolt and the defiance and their replacement with a recognition of the correctness of the decision as a valid, constitutional affirmation of American values. But this has not happened with the decision in *Roe* v. *Wade*. Even after the passage of almost thirty years, it continued to divide public opinion, to divide political parties and candidates for public office, and played a role, overt or covert, in nominations for judicial positions.

The case involves many issues and problems that are important but are not germane to our inquiry, which is the historical development of the concept of fundamental rights in American constitutional law. Concentration on this aspect of the case suffices to expose deep cleavages in constitutional theory.

Roe v. *Wade* was decided by a vote of 7–2. In addition to the opinion for the Court by Justice Blackmun, there were three concurring and two dissenting opinions. We shall examine the opinions only in so far as they have a bearing on the concept or doctrine of fundamental rights.

The opinion for the Court divided pregnancy into trimesters and held that during the first trimester the woman, in consultation with her physician, had a virtually unrestricted right to choose abortion. Restrictions on that right were unconstitutional. During the second trimester, when abortion posed a threat to the woman's health, the States could regulate abortions to protect her health. In the third trimester, the State had a legitimate interest in protecting the potential life of the fetus, and this interest was sufficiently great enough to warrant severe restrictions on abortion; however, even so, the State must permit abortion to save the woman's life.

Justice Blackmun acknowledges that "The Constitution does not explicitly mention any right of privacy." Nonetheless, the Court in a variety of cases has recognized "that a right of personal privacy, or a guarantee of certain areas or zones of privacy, does exist under the Constitution." The Court cited some cases, including *Griswold* and *Meyer*. The cited decisions, said Justice Blackmun, make it clear that "only personal rights that can be deemed 'fundamental' or 'implicit in the concept of ordered liberty,' *Palko* v. *Connecticut*, . . . are included in this guarantee of personal privacy." Then Justice Blackmun enumerated the personal rights that have been held to be included in the guarantee: activities relating to marriage, procreation, contraception, child rearing and education, citing, inter alia, *Pierce* and *Meyer*. "This right of privacy, whether it be founded in the Fourteenth Amendment's concept of personal liberty and restrictions upon state action, as we feel it is, or, . . . in the Ninth Amendment's reservation of rights to the people, is broad enough to encompass a woman's decision whether or not to terminate her pregnancy."

Having decided that a woman has the *fundamental right* to choose an abortion, guaranteed by the Due Process Clause of the Fourteenth Amendment (within the conditions defined by the Court in the trimester schedule), the opinion went on to say that a State's regulation limiting this *fundamental right* "may be justified only by a 'compelling interest,'" and that statutes "must be narrowly drawn to express only the legitimate state interests at stake."

In his dissenting opinion, Justice Rehnquist said that he failed to see any thing "private" in abortion. He said that he agreed that the term "liberty" in the Due Process Clause "embraces more than the rights found in the Bill of Rights," but enjoyment of that "liberty" is guaranteed only against deprivation without due process of law, and when the area of the deprivation is social or economic legislation, then the test of constitutionality is whether the statute "has a rational relation to a valid state objective." This is the established test that should apply to the abortion statutes.

What Justice Rehnquist said essentially is that a woman's right to an abortion is not a fundamental right; it is a right that is subject to regulation by the State, and such regulation falls into the area of social legislation, which is presumed to be constitutional. The person challenging such a statute must show that there is no rational ground that could sustain it.

Justice White, in his brief dissenting opinion, said that he found nothing in the history of the Constitution that would support the majority decision. The legislature of a State is entitled to weigh the relative importance of the continued existence and development of the fetus against a "spectrum of possible impacts on the mother." The Court, however, "values the convenience of the pregnant mother more than the continued existence and development of the life or potential life that she carries." But there is no constitutional warrant for the Court imposing such an order of priorities on the people and legislature of a State.

Roe v. *Wade* was decided by a Court majority of seven Justices that included three who had been appointed by President Nixon; namely, Justices Blackmun, Powell, and Chief Justice Burger; yet ironically, the most liberal of the Burger Court decisions and the one most widely and most deeply attacked by conservatives was the abortion decision. Of President Nixon's appointees, only Justice Rehnquist dissented, and the other dissenting Justice, Justice White, had been appointed by President Kennedy, a liberal.

A case in which a majority of the Court adhered firmly to the rationale of *Roe* v. *Wade* was *Thornburgh* v. *American College of Obstetricians and Gynecologists*,[34] decided in 1986. By vote of 5–4 the Court invalidated a number of abortion regulations of Pennsylvania. In an opinion by Justice Blackmun, the Court held that the Pennsylvania statute subordinated the constitutional privacy right of the pregnant woman to an effort by the State to deter her from making a decision that, with her physician, was hers alone to make. The statute required that the woman be given information that was designed to influence her against the choice of an abortion; the statute required the reporting of certain information, that would be available to the public, and could expose her to harassment; there was a requirement for a second physician being present, but there was no requirement that there be a showing of a medical emergency.

Chief Justice Burger dissented because he thought that the Court was going too far in a direction that was contrary to our history and tradition. If this is what the majority meant by the right to an abortion, then, said Chief Justice Burger, "I agree we should reexamine *Roe*."

Justice O'Connor, with Justice Rehnquist joining, dissented in a long opinion. Besides referring to the trimester framework as "outmoded," her opinion is interesting to us for her contention that the State has compelling interests in ensuring the maternal health of the pregnant woman *and* in protecting potential life, and these interests exist throughout pregnancy (that is, in each of the trimesters). There is a strong implication in this dissenting opinion that the Pennsylvania requirements could pass the strict scrutiny test, but here the majority have devised a new rule, i. e., that "the mere possibility that some women will be less likely to choose to have an abortion by virtue of the presence of a particular state regulation suffices to invalidate it." Judicial scrutiny of abortion regulations, she said, "should be limited to whether the state law bears a rational relationship to legitimate purposes . . . , with heightened scrutiny reserved for instances in which the State has imposed an 'undue burden' on the abortion decision."

Justice O'Connor's opinion is far from being crystal clear. The fact that Justice Rehnquist joined her opinion lends some strength to the reading that she believed that the right to choose an abortion is not a fundamental right, that it is a right that the State may regulate at every stage of pregnancy, and that regulations need not satisfy the strict scrutiny test, but a new test that she has propounded. This, I think, comes very close to overruling *Roe*. As we shall see, a later case validates this reading of her opinion.

And this is precisely what was said by Justice White in his dissenting opinion, which Justice Rehnquist joined. "In my view," he wrote, "the time has come [to hold] that *Roe* v. *Wade* . . . 'departs from a proper understanding' of the Constitution and to overrule it." He said that he agreed that a woman's ability to choose an abortion is a species of "liberty" that is "subject to the general protections of the Due Process Clause," but he could not agree that this is a "fundamental" right so that "restrictions upon it call into play anything more than the most minimal judicial scrutiny." The right to choose an abortion is not "implicit in the concept of ordered liberty," nor is it "deeply rooted in this Nation's history and traditions." The State has an interest in protecting "those who will be citizens if their lives are not ended in the womb," and this interest is "compelling" at viability and before viability (that is, in each of the trimesters).

Thus in 1986, in *Thornburgh*, certainly three, and possibly three and 3/4ths of the Justices were ready to overrule *Roe* and to decide that a woman's right to choose an abortion is not a *fundamental* right under the Due Process Clause.

Three years later the Court had before it *Webster* v. *Reproductive Health Services*.[35] In the years between these two decisions, Chief Justice Burger was replaced by Justice Rehnquist as Chief Justice, and Antonin Scalia was named Associate Justice. Justice Powell resigned and Anthony M. Kennedy took his place. Both Justices Scalia and Kennedy were appointed by President Reagan.

For reasons unknown, *Webster* excited almost as much public, political excitement as did *Roe*. Although it hardly effected any serious change in the law relating to abortion, *Webster* stimulated the so-called right-to-life proponents to pressure State legislatures to further restrict abortion rights, while proponents of such rights saw in *Webster* a major threat to successful litigation in support of *Roe*. In reality, however, the decision hardly merited the notoriety and the heat that it generated.

The case was decided by a 5–4 vote. The plurality opinion was by Chief Justice Rehnquist, with concurring opinions by Justices Scalia and O'Connor. Justice Blackmun dissented in an opinion joined by Justices Brennan and Marshall, and Justice Stevens also dissented. The mere fact that the Court upheld some restrictions on abortion, the mere fact that Justice Blackmun, author of the Court's opinion in *Roe*, had to dissent, were apparently sufficient causes for satisfaction and alarm.

A preamble to the Missouri statute stated that life begins at conception. The Court held that the preamble was merely precatory, so that its validity was not before the Court. A provision of the law was that no state property may be used for an abortion, the effect of which was to bar use of state-supported hospitals even if the patient paid for the service. The Court held that the provision was indistinguishable from the prohibition on use of public funds for abortions that was upheld in *Harris* v. *McRae*,[36] decided nine years before.

A major provision of the Missouri law was that physicians were required to perform tests to determine the viability of the fetus in cases where, in the physician's judgment, the fetus was twenty or more weeks old. According to *Roe*, this meant that the pregnancy was in the second trimester, and in that case *Roe* held that a regulation is lawful only to assure the woman's health. The Court upheld the Missouri regulation by modifying *Roe*. Chief Justice Rehnquist said that while a woman has a "liberty" interest in choosing an abortion, guaranteed by the Due Process Clause, the State had an interest in protecting the viability or life of the fetus, and this interest pervaded throughout the pregnancy (and not only in the third trimester as was held in *Roe*). The clear implication in this holding is that a State may regulate abortions in the interest of the fetus throughout the nine months and not only in the last three months of the pregnancy, and thus may even go so far as to criminalize any abortion. But the plurality opinion, foreseeing such an interpretation, said that it disclaimed approval of a return to a time when such severe restrictions on abortions existed.

The Court, then, it appears, modified *Roe* in an important respect but stopped short of overruling it. Justice Scalia, however, would not only have voted to overrule *Roe*, but took the plurality to task for failing to do so.

The logic of the Court is difficult to follow. If the choosing of an abortion is a woman's fundamental right, then the guarantee of this right is meaningful only if any restriction or regulation is subject to strict scrutiny. This species of judicial review is its only protection. If this is true of, e. g., freedom of speech, which is a fundamental right, it is equally true of any other fundamental right. Once it is held that the State has an interest in the "life" of the fetus at any stage of its development, equal to an interest in the life of the woman, and if any regulation of abortion is subject to a test weaker than strict scrutiny, it is meaningless to say that the woman has a fundamental right to an abortion. She has a right within the meaning of "liberty" guaranteed by the Due Process Clause, but not a right that is fundamental. In effect, the holding of *Roe* v. *Wade* has been whittled away; an outright overruling may not make a meaningful difference.

There is little point in examining each of the many cases on abortion that have been decided, that only add, one after another victory for the anti-*Roe* forces; but it may be helpful to see how muddied the waters have become by considering a case decided in 1992, *Planned parenthood v. Casey*,[37] in which there was no majority opinion and in which there were five long opinions.

VI.

Provisions of a Pennsylvania act, adopted in 1988 and 1989, require a woman to delay an abortion for twenty-four hours and to listen to a

State-sponsored lecture. It requires a minor to obtain the informed consent of at least one parent or, alternatively, a court order certifying that she is "mature" enough to give informed consent or that abortion would be in her best interest. It also provides that a married woman must notify her husband of her intention to have an abortion. There is also a provision relating to an emergency, there are detailed reporting requirements on physicians and on facilities that provide abortion services.

In a very long opinion of which there are three authors—Justices O'Connor, Kennedy, and Souter—that represents the judgment of the Court, it is noted, in the opening paragraph, that it was nineteen years since the decision in *Roe*, that the Constitution protects a woman's right to terminate her pregnancy in its early stages, but that "that definition of liberty is still questioned," and that joining in the argument to support the State's regulations is the United States that now, for the sixth time, asks the Court to overrule *Roe*.

A large portion of the joint opinion is devoted to argument why *Roe* ought not to be overruled. The opinion elaborates a philosophy of *stare decisis* that reads more like a chapter in a textbook on jurisprudence than part of a judicial opinion. The tone of this part of the opinion is definitely a defensive one; it virtually apologizes for not overruling *Roe*. The tone, the spirit of the opinion bring *Roe* to the very brink of discarding, of toppling it.

Having decided not to overrule *Roe*, the joint opinion finally gets around to stating what it is in *Roe* that it finds acceptable. The first point it makes is the following:

> The woman's right to terminate her pregnancy before viability is the most central principle of *Roe v. Wade*. It is a rule of law and a component of liberty we cannot renounce.

It is to be noted that neither at this point, nor at any other point in the entire joint opinion, is the "right" denominated a "fundamental right." This, I submit, is very crucial, for what is only a right is only a naked right; it has only minimum protection against legislative regulation, control by the State's exercise of its police power. Not to recognize a woman's right to an abortion as a *fundament right* is to take the heart out of *Roe*. For *Roe*, in the Court's opinion by Justice Blackmun, squarely placed the right to an abortion within the fundamental right of privacy. That opinion, after citing *Griswold*, *Meyer* and several other decisions, stated:

These decisions make it clear that only personal rights that can be deemed "fundamental" or "implicit in the concept of ordered liberty", *Palko* v. *Connecticut*, . . . are
included in this guarantee of personal privacy. . . .
   This right of privacy . . . is broad enough to encompass a woman's decision
whether or not to terminate her pregnancy.

Once a decision is made to downgrade the right to an abortion from
being a fundamental right to a mere right, it is easy to remove from
Roe its important features, so that in the end it is hardly recognizable.
This is precisely what the joint opinion proceeded to do.

I think it is safe to say that until the *Casey* decision was handed
down, anyone familiar with *Roe* would have thought that the trimester
schedule was one of its most essential components. But this is what
the joint opinion decided: "We reject the trimester framework, which
we do not consider to be part of the essential holding of *Roe*."

The point of the trimester framework was to place the first trimester
beyond the reach of the legislature. In the first trimester the woman, in
consultation with her physician, had the right to decide, without interference from any legislative action, to have an abortion. There were no
so-called rights of the unborn that could be an impediment to her
exercise of the right to an abortion. The unborn's "rights" can be
asserted only when the fetus becomes viable. But the joint opinion
subverts the decision of *Roe* and holds that the State has a legitimate
interest not only in the health of the woman, but also in the potential
life of the fetus, throughout her pregnancy, from its very beginning.
Said the joint opinion:

Even in the earliest stages of pregnancy, the State may enact rules and regulations
designed to encourage her to know that there are philosophic and social arguments
of great weight that can be brought to bear in favor of continuing the pregnancy to
full term and that there are procedures and institutions to allow adoption of un-
wanted children as well as a certain degree of state assistance if the mother chooses
to raise the child herself. . . . It follows that States are free to enact laws to provide
a reasonable framework for a woman to make a decision that has such profound
and lasting meaning. This, too, we find consistent with *Roe's* central premises, and
indeed the inevitable consequence of our holding that the State has an interest in
protecting the life of the unborn.

Yes, the State has an interest in protecting the life of the unborn, but
according to *Roe* that interest does not arise before viability. Said the
Court in *Roe*: "With respect to the State's important and legitimate
interest in potential life, the 'compelling' point is at viability." This is

at the third trimester, not at the first. The Court in *Roe* said: "Where certain 'fundamental rights, are involved, the Court has held that regulation limiting these rights may be justified only by a 'compelling state interest.'" How the joint opinion in *Casey* could allow itself to claim that what it says was "consistent with *Roe's* central premises" was like saying that black is white.

Since, says the joint opinion, "there is a substantial state interest in potential life throughout pregnancy," it follows that "not all regulations must be deemed unwarranted. Not all burdens on the right to decide whether to terminate a pregnancy will be undue." One would naturally expect that the test would be rationality, or rational basis scrutiny, or possibly an intermediate level of scrutiny, such as is applied in cable television cases[38] that gives recognition, on the one hand, to the commercial aspect in the facts of the case, and, on the other hand, to the First Amendment speech aspect. Well, the joint opinion does come up with a sort-of intermediate test that it refers to as an "undue burden" test. What is that test? The answer is as follows:

> A finding of an undue burden is a shorthand for the conclusion that a state regulation has the purpose or effect of placing a substantial obstacle in the path of a woman seeking an abortion of a nonviolable fetus. A statute with this purpose is invalid because the means chosen by the State to further the interest in potential life must be calculated to inform the woman's free choice, not hinder it.

This test was first propounded by Justice O'Connor.[39]

Subjecting the Pennsylvania regulations to this test, the joint opinion upheld as constitutional all but the provision requiring the reporting of failure to provide spousal notice. This provision, the opinion says, violated the Due Process Clause by placing an undue burden on a woman's choice. "This conclusion," said the joint opinion, "is in no way inconsistent with our decisions upholding parental notification or consent requirements." The nub of the difference is that between minor women and adult women, for a minor will benefit from consultation with her parents, who have the best interests of children at heart, but the Justices "cannot adopt a parallel assumption about adult women." Why is it not equally reasonable that a woman will benefit from consultation with her husband and that a husband has her best interests at heart?

Justice Stevens concurred except that he found the following additional requirements invalid: (a) the requirement that the woman be provided with materials that are designed to persuade her not to undergo an abortion, and (b) the 24-hour waiting period. Justice Blackmun concurred and dissented. He would hold all the requirements unconstitutional under the strict scrutiny test and under the principle of stare decisis. He said that the trimester framework ought not to be disturbed. He, however, concurred to the limited extent of upholding as valid the medical emergency provision. Justice Blackmun consoled himself with the fact that the joint opinion states that "the essential holding of *Roe* v. *Wade* should be retained and once again reaffirmed," and that Justice Stevens accepted this proposition, so that five Justices (including himself) subscribe to this holding.

At the start of his opinion, Justice Blackmun with unhidden pathos, wrote: "And I fear for the darkness [the overruling of *Roe*] as four [dissenting] Justices anxiously await the single vote necessary to extinguish the light [that came with *Roe*]." And he concluded on the same pathetic note. The distance between the majority and the dissenting Justices is short—

the distance is but a single vote.
    I am 83 years old. I cannot remain on this Court forever, and when I do step down, the confirmation process for my successor well may focus on the issue before us today. That, I regret, may be exactly where the choice between the two worlds will be made.

The two dissenting opinions, by Chief Justice Rehnquist and by Justice Scalia, each of which was joined by Justices White and Thomas, were written with an unusual quantity of fire and brimstone. Each accused the joint opinion of intellectual dishonesty and perverse logic. The joint opinion while retaining "the outer shell" of *Roe*, "beats a wholesale retreat from the substance of that case." They wrote that *Roe* should be overruled, and they upheld all of the provisions of the Pennsylvania statute. There is no support in our history, wrote the Chief Justice, for the holding in *Roe* that the right to an abortion is a "fundamental" right. There is no support, he said, in *Griswold*, or *Meyer*, or *Pierce* for the decision in *Roe* that abortion is a fundamental right guaranteed by the Fourteenth Amendment.

The joint opinion, Chief Justice Rehnquist wrote, rejects the view that a woman has a fundamental right to an abortion. The joint opinion rejects the view that abortion regulations were to be subjected to strict scrutiny. The joint opinion rejects the trimester framework. "*Roe* continues to exist, but only in the way a storefront on a western movie set exists: a mere facade to give the illusion of reality." And behind the facade, said the Chief Justice, there stands "an entirely new method of analysis [the 'undue burden standard'] without any roots in constitutional law." Abortion regulations are not subject to heightened scrutiny but to the test of rationality, and when so tested, the regulations before the Court were constitutional in their entirety.

Justice Scalia wrote that the joint opinion did not defend the "real" *Roe* v. *Wade*, but rather a "fabricated version" of which the Justices were the authors. He describes the "undue burden" test as "amorphous," as an invention of Justice O'Connor that is "inherently manipulable" and "hopelessly unworkable in practice." It has no "principled or coherent legal basis." Justice Scalia characterizes the arguments in the joint opinion as "outrageous," the worst of which "it is beyond human nature to leave unanswered."

Before we leave *Casey* it is, I think, important to note that, in his dissenting opinion, Chief Justice Rehnquist went so far as to deny that there is a general "all-encompassing 'right of privacy.'" There are certain rights that come "under the rubric of personal or family privacy and autonomy," that the Court has protected, but not any "all-encompassing 'right of privacy.'" What are the rights included in the "rubric" that the Court has protected? Chief Justice Rehnquist listed the following, citing *Pierce*, *Meyer*, *Griswold*, and several other cases: a parent's right to send a child to a private school, a right to teach a foreign language in a parochial school, a right to marry, a right to procreate, and a right to use contraceptives. One can assume, from various statements in the opinion, that Chief Justice Rehnquist would concede that these are fundamental rights. But abortion is sui generis, it is different in kind from the others, and is, therefore, not protected to the same degree or in the same way. It does not fall under the rubric of personal or family privacy and autonomy. It is, I think, reasonable to assume that Justices White, Scalia, and Thomas, who joined in the dissent, agreed with the Chief Justice on these propositions.

Looking at *Casey* in its totality, it appears that the entire Court—except Justice Blackmun—agreed that abortion is not a fundamental right. Regulations of the right to an abortion are not subject to strict scrutiny. *Roe* v. *Wade* still has some form of existence, but that of a ghost and not of a being of flesh and bones.

Abortion is the second fundamental right to have been nullified.

The first, the liberty of contract, was nullified in 1937 with the end of the *Lochner* era.[40]

Since *Casey*, Justices White and Blackmun have retired and have been replaced by Justices Ruth Bader Ginsburg and Stephen Breyer. But these changes are unlikely to affect the future of the right of choice to have an abortion. For the foreseeable years *Roe* v. *Wade* is likely to continue its spectral—unenviable—existence.

VII.

In his dissenting opinion in *Casey*, Justice Scalia said that he reached the conclusion that the right of a woman to an abortion is not a liberty protected by the Constitution "for the same reason" that he would have to reach the conclusion "that bigamy is not constitutionally protected—because of two simple facts: (1) the Constitution says absolutely nothing about it, and (2) the longstanding traditions of American society have permitted it to be legally proscribed." Three months before Antonin Scalia took his place as a Justice of the Supreme Court, the Court voted on the question whether the act of sodomy is constitutionally protected. Had he participated in the case of *Bowers* v. *Hardwick*,[41] he probably would have made the identical point—that sodomy, like abortion, like bigamy, is not protected by the Constitution, because it is not mentioned in the Constitution, and because the longstanding traditions of American society have permitted it to be legally proscribed.

A Georgia statute made it a criminal offense to commit sodomy. The act was punishable by up to twenty years imprisonment. A homosexual was charged with violating the statute by committing sodomy with a consenting male in the bedroom of his home. The district attorney had decided not to prosecute, but the homosexual brought suit in a Federal District Court challenging the constitutionality of the statute; the court dismissed the action; the Court of Appeals, however, reversed and remanded for trial, holding that the statute violated the homosexual's fundamental right to privacy, guaranteed by the Due Process Clause, and that the State, in order to prevail, had to prove that it had a compelling interest in prohibiting such behavior, and that the statute was the most narrowly drawn means of achieving that end. The case was appealed to the Supreme Court.

The judgment was reversed. Justice White wrote the opinion for five members of the Court. Justices Blackmun, Stevens, Brennan, and Marshall dissented.

In his opinion for the Court, Justice White (joined by Chief Justice Burger and Justices Powell, Rehnquist, and O'Connor), said that sodomy was a criminal offense at common law, was forbidden in the thirteen original States when they ratified the Bill of Rights, and that when the Fourteenth Amendment was ratified in 1868, all but five of the States had criminal sodomy laws; that until 1961, all fifty States outlawed sodomy, and that at the time of the decision, twenty-five States and the District of Columbia had criminal sodomy laws. "Against this background," said the Court, "to claim that a right to engage in such conduct is 'deeply rooted in this Nation's history and tradition,' or 'implicit in the concept of ordered liberty' is, at best, facetious."

Facetious though the claim might be, the Court nonetheless faced the claim seriously. The majority opinion rejected the argument that previous decisions in the realm of privacy had implicitly decided that sodomy was a fundamental right, and went on to say that the Court is not inclined to discover new fundamental rights in the Due Process Clause. There should be, said Justice White, "great resistance to expand the substantive reach of those [Due Process] Clauses particularly if it requires redefining the category of rights deemed to be fundamental."

Justice White rejected the argument that the sodomy statute is unconstitutional as an illegal invasion of the privacy of the homosexual's home just as it had held, in *Stanley* v. *Georgia*,[42] that the First Amendment prevents conviction for possessing and reading obscene material in the privacy of one's home. But that case, said Justice White, had support in the text of the Constitution, i. e., in the First Amendment. Sodomy has no such support in the text of the Fourteenth Amendment. *Stanley* offers no protection for the commission of crimes in one's home, such as the possession of drugs, firearms, stolen goods—or sodomy. And if sodomy were permitted, if committed in one's home, what of adultery, incest, and other sexual crimes? "We are unwilling to start down that road."

The argument was made that the statute is unconstitutional even if sodomy may not be a fundamental right, for it has no rational basis other than the presumed belief of a majority of the people of Georgia that homosexual sodomy is immoral, and this is inadequate reason for criminalizing the conduct. "The law, however," said Justice White, "is constantly based on notions of morality, and if all laws representing essentially moral choices are to be invalidated under the Due Process Clause, the courts will be very busy indeed."

In his dissenting opinion, Justice Blackmun (with whom were joined Justices Brennan, Marshall, and Stevens), contended that the case was not about "a fundamental right to engage in homosexual sodomy," nor was *Stanley* "about a fundamental right to watch obscene movies," rather, he said, the case was about—in the words of Justice Brandeis— "the most comprehensive of rights and the right most valued by civilized men," namely, "the right to be let alone." How is one to define this right? Justice Blackmun said that the case involves the claim that the statute "interferes with constitutionally protected interests in privacy and freedom of intimate association." But this only injects other terms that need to be defined. They are not themselves definitions.

Justice Blackmun said that the Court's decisions construing the right of privacy have proceeded along two lines. First, there are decisions that have recognized "a privacy interest" with reference to certain decisions that are properly for the individual to make. The instant case involves such a decision. Justice Blackmun interprets certain cases from this point of view. (a) Cases that the Court's opinion characterizes by their connection to protection of the family. But the Court's conclusion that these cases extend no further is a misreading of their true rationale. The family is protected because the rights connected with it form a central part of an individual's life. The decision to marry is protected because marriage "'is an association that promotes a way of life, not a cause; a harmony in living, not political faiths; a bilateral loyalty, not commercial or social projects.'" The decision whether to have a child is protected "because parenthood alters so dramatically an individual's self definition, not because of demographic considerations or the Bible's command to be fruitful and multiply." "And we protect the family because it contributes so powerfully to the happiness of individuals, not because of a preference for stereotypical households." The opinion mentions the "ability independently to define one's identity that is central to any concept of liberty." (b) Cases with respect to sex. Sexual intimacy, the dissenting opinion says, is "'a sensitive, key relationship of human existence, central to family life, community welfare, and the development of human personality.'" Individuals define themselves in a significant way through their intimate sexual relationships. In a Nation as diverse as is ours, "there may be many 'right' ways of conducting those relationships." Much of the richness of a relationship will come "from the freedom an individual has to *choose* the form and nature of these intensely personal bonds." (Emphasis in original.) The fact is that "different individuals will make different choices." "'A way of life that is odd or even erratic but interferes with no rights or interests of others is not to be condemned because it is different.'" Concluding this section of the dissenting opinion, Justice Blackmun wrote:

> The Court claims that its decision today merely refuses to recognize a fundamental right to engage in homosexual sodomy; what the Court really has refused to recognize is the fundamental interest all individuals have in controlling the nature of their intimate associations with others.

Second, Justice Blackmun considered the place where the conduct happened. With respect to this phase of the case, too, the Court, said Justice Blackmun, refused to place the specific cases of privacy under broad principles. He wrote:

> Just as the right to privacy is more than the mere aggregation of a number of entitlements to engage in specific behavior, so, too, protecting the physical integrity of the home is more than merely a means of protecting specific activities that often take place there.

What are the broad principles? Quoting the first Justice Harlan, Justice Blackmun wrote: "the essence of a Fourth Amendment violation is 'not the breaking of [a person's] doors, and the rummaging of his drawers,' but rather is 'the invasion of his indefeasible right of personal security, personal liberty and private property.'" Justice Blackmun contested the Court's interpretation of *Stanley* as resting on the First Amendment right to read or view obscene materials in the privacy of one's home; rather, according to the dissenting opinion, it rested on the Fourth Amendment's special protection for the individual in his home. Indeed, the Fourth Amendment is "perhaps the most 'textual' of the various constitutional provisions that inform our understanding of the right to privacy. . . . Indeed, the right of an individual to conduct intimate relationships in the intimacy of his or her own home seems to me to be the heart of the Constitution's protection of privacy."

Both Justices Blackmun and Stevens, each in his own dissenting opinion, point out that the Georgia statute was not explicitly directed against homosexuals but against acts of sodomy whether committed by homosexuals or by heterosexuals; the majority, however, chose to disregard this fact and concentrated entirely on the fact that the case involved an act of sodomy by homosexuals. Justice Blackmun called attention to this fact in a footnote and only briefly suggested constitutional lines of argument emanating from it, but Justice Stevens, with Justices Brennan and Marshall joining, argued elaborately that the Court's privacy precedents would clearly lead to the conclusion that acts of sodomy between married or unmarried heterosexual adults are protected. If this is the case, then singling out homosexuals for prosecution raises serious questions under the Equal Protection Clause. Since the statute, as written, cannot be used against heterosexuals, then the State has the burden of justifying a selective—discriminatory—application of the law. In any case, said Justice Stevens,

> the homosexual and the heterosexual have the same interest in deciding how he will live his own life, and, more narrowly, how he will conduct himself in his personal and voluntary associations with his companions. State intrusion into the private conduct of either is equally burdensome.

The claim by Justice White that the right of privacy was limited to the cases previously decided, it seems to me, makes all of the privacy decisions unprincipled. They become, as Justice Blackmun rightly said, a mere aggregation of cases, only arbitrarily placed under a common rubric. If one is asked what is the right of privacy, the Court would answer by only citing previous decisions, each of which was an *ad hoc* decision. Like verdicts of a jury on the facts, that cannot be used as precedents, the privacy cases previously decided have no status as precedents, one cannot move from them to other factual situations, because no general principle can be cited as their *ratio decidendi*. Surely the fact that there were laws against sodomy hundreds of years ago cannot serve as a foundation in constitutional law, for, as Justice Holmes said (a quotation used by Justice Blackmun), "[i]t is revolting to have no better reason for a rule of law than that so it was laid down in the time of Henry IV." Nor is the fact that there are laws against sodomy in many or most of the States persuasive as a principle. The fact that miscegenation was outlawed in many States did not keep the Court from declaring such laws unconstitutional.

If the Court were to uphold the right of homosexuals to engage in acts of sodomy in the privacy of one's bedroom, then, the Court asked, what about adultery and incest committed in the home? "We are unwilling," wrote Justice White, "to start down that road." This is the slippery-pole argument. It is a notorious logical fallacy. When this type of argument was used in a tax case, Justice Holmes answered it with the statement that has become famous: "The power to tax is not the power to destroy while this Court sits."[43] Justice Blackmun, in a footnote, pointed out that there are important differences between, on the one hand, homosexual acts of sodomy and, on the other hand, adultery and incest. Nothing in the Constitution requires the law to treat equally things that are different.[44] "Neither are we troubled," wrote Justice Holmes, "by the question where to draw the line. That is the question in pretty much everything worth arguing in the law."[45]

By narrowing the holding of the Court in *Pierce, Meyer, Griswold*, et al., to just the facts in each case, Justice White emasculated these seminal decisions. They are left as if they were like jury verdicts, decisions merely on the facts. It is as if there were no opinions at all in the cases, but only judgments. This is, I submit, a denigration of the Court. It is a disregarding of the warning of Chief Justice Marshall: "We must never forget that it is a *constitution* we are expounding." (Emphasis in original.)[46]

When writing his opinion in *Bowers*, Justice White apparently forgot what he had himself written in his concurring opinion in *Griswold*. In that opinion he wrote: "in my view this Connecticut law [making the use of contraceptives a criminal offense] as applied to married couples deprives them of 'liberty' without due process of law, as that concept is used in the Fourteenth Amendment." He identified the Connecticut statute as one that regulated "sensitive areas of liberty." As such, the statute had to be subjected to "strict scrutiny." The privacy involved in that case was not based, by Justice White, on the protection of one's home by the Fourth Amendment; it was given a much wider scope of protection by being placed under the much wider guarantee of "liberty" as provided by the Fourteenth Amendment. In a footnote in his *Griswold* concurring opinion, Justice White attacked the attempt by the dissenting Justices to give a narrow interpretation of the Due Process Clause. "The traditional due process test," he wrote, "was well articulated and applied in . . . a case which placed no reliance on the specific guarantees of the Bill of Rights."

I think that the majority of the Court in *Bowers* silently denied that there is such a constitutional right as privacy. Yes, admittedly, there is the decision invalidating the anti-contraceptive statute, but that does not spell out a fundamental right of privacy as a "liberty" protected by the Due Process Clause. Essentially, in the twenty-one years between *Griswold* and *Bowers*, the Court had moved away from the opinion by Justice White in the former case to the dissenting opinion of Justice Black. It will be remembered that Justice Black refused to acknowledge that there are any constitutional rights or liberties except those explicitly enumerated in the Bill of Rights or anywhere else in the Constitution. "Privacy" is not mentioned in the Constitution; therefore, it does not exist. "The Court," wrote Justice Black, "talks about a constitutional 'right of privacy' as though there is some constitutional provision or provisions forbidding any law ever to be passed which might abridge the 'privacy' of individuals. But there is not." The Court must, he said, stick to "the simple language" of the Constitution. Justice Black deprecated such cases as *Pierce* and *Meyer* as based on "the same natural law due process philosophy . . . which I cannot accept." "I cannot rely," wrote Justice Black, "on the Due Process Clause or . . . any mysterious and uncertain natural law concept as a reason for striking down this state law."

As we noted, *Bowers* v. *Hardwick* was decided by a 5–4 vote. Justice Powell is said to have been the crucial swing vote. In October 1990, in a talk to students at New York University, he said that he "probably made a mistake" in voting as he did.[47]

In their joint opinion in *Casey*, the Justices wrote that the "Court must take care to speak and act in ways that allow people to accept its decisions on the terms the Court claims for them, as grounded truly in principle. . . ." The Court's legitimacy, they said, "depends on making legally principled decisions under circumstances in which their principled character is sufficiently plausible to be accepted by the Nation." One may say that this is nicely put as a pious hope but unfortunately fails as a true description of what the Court has consistently done. In the very case in which this was said there was not even a plurality, let alone a majority, opinion, but only a "joint opinion" written ostensibly by three Justices.

No shining principles stand out as the Court implicitly, but not overtly, overrules *Roe* v. *Wade*, and, in *Bowers* v. *Hardwick*, fails to acknowledge that there is, indeed, a fundamental right to privacy, and in neither case is there a principled Court's opinion that makes it "sufficiently plausible to be accepted by the Nation."

Notes

1. *Corfield* v. *Coryell*, 6 Fed. Cas. 546 (1823).
2. *Slaughter-Houses Cases*, 16 Wall. (83 U.S.) 36 (1873), opinion of Justice Field, dissenting.
3. *O'Neil* v. *Vermont*, 144 U.S. 323 (1892), dissenting opinion.
4. *Twining* v. *New Jersey*, 211 U.S. 78 (1908), dissenting opinion.
5. *Meyer* v. *Nebraska*, 262 U.S. 390 (1923).
6. *Pierce* v. *Society of Sisters*, 268 U.S. 510 (1925).
7. *Palko* v. *Connecticut*, 302 U.S. 319 (1937).
8. *Benton* v. *Maryland*, 395 U.S. 784 (1969).
9. *Slaughter-House Cases*, 16 Wall (83 U.S.) 36 (1873).
10. *Allgeyer* v. *Louisiana*, 165 U.S. 578 (1897).
11. *Lochner* v. *New York*, 198 U.S. 45 (1905). Italics supplied.
12. Benj. Wright, *The Growth of American Constitutional Law* (1942), 154, 176. For comprehensive list of State acts and municipal ordinances held unconstitutional on various grounds, see *The Constitution of the United States*, Congressional Research Service, Library of Congress (Washington, D.C., 1987), 1915–2113.
13. *West Coast Hotel* v. *Parrish*, 300 U.S. 379 (1937); *United States* v. *Darby*, 312 U.S. 100 (1941); *NLRB* v. *Jones & Laughlin Steel Co.*, 301 U.S. 1 (1937); *Wickard* v. *Filburn*, 317 U.S. 111 (1942).
14. *Lincoln Federal Labor Union* v. *Northwestern Iron and Metal Co.*, 335 U.S. 525 (1949).
15. *Griswold* v. *Connecticut*, 381 U.S. 479 (1965).
16. *Pierce* v. *Society of Sisters*, 268 U.S. 510 (1925).
17. *Meyer* v. *Nebraska*, 262 U.S. 390 (1923).
18. Citing *NAACP* v. *Alabama*, 357 U.S. 449 (1958).
19. Quotation from *Snyder* v. *Massachusetts*, 291 U.S. 91 (1934).
20. *Gitlow* v. *New York*, 268 U.S. 652 (1925).
21. *Barron* v. *Baltimore*, 32 U.S. 243 (1833).
22. Justice White, in a concurring opinion avoided discussion of the question of incorporation or of fundamental rights but attacked the statute as being overly broad.
23. *Moore* v. *East Cleveland*, 431 U.S. 494 (1977). Italics supplied.
24. *Poe* v. *Ullman*, 167 U.S. 497 (1961), dissenting opinion. Italics supplied.
25. *Duncan* v. *Louisiana*, 391 U.S. 145 (1968).
26. *Roe* v. *Wade*, 410 U.S. 113 (1973).
27. *Whitney* v. *Calif.*, 274 U.S. 357 (1927).
28. Italics in original.
29. *Kelley* v. *Johnson*, 425 U.S. 238 (1976).
30. *Meachum* v. *Fano*, 427 U.S. 215 (1976).
31. *Albright* v. *Oliver*, 127 L Ed 2d 114 (1994).
32. *Dolan* v. *City of Tigard*, 129 L Ed 2d 304 (1994).
33. *Brown* v. *Board of Education*, 347 U.S. 483 (1954).
34. *Thornburgh* v. *American College of Obstetricians and Gynecologists*, 476 U.S. 747 (1986).
35. *Webster* v. *Reproductive Health Services*, 492 U.S. 490 (1989).
36. *Harris* v. *McRae*, 448 U.S. 297 (1980).
37. *Planned Parenthood* v. *Casey*, 120 L Ed 2d 674 (1992).
38. *Turner Broadcasting Co.* v. *FCC*, 129 L Ed 2d 497 (1994).

39. *Ohio* v. *Akron Center for Reproductive Health*, 497 U.S. 502 (1990), dis. op. Justice O'Connor.
40. *West Coast Hotel Co.* v. *Parrish.* 300 U.S. 379 (1937).
41. *Bowers* v. *Hardwick*, 478 U.S. 186 (1986).
42. *Stanley* v. *Georgia*, 394 U.S. 557 (1969).
43. *Panhandle Oil Co.* v. *Mississippi*, 277 U.S. 218 (1928).
44. Justice Stone in *Puget Sound Power & Light Co.* v. *Seattle*, 291 U.S. 619, 624 (1934).
45. *Irwin* v. *Gavit*, 268 U.S. 161, 168 (1925).
46. *McCulloch* v. *Maryland*, 4 Wheat. 316, 407 (1819).
47. K. L. Hall, ed., *Oxford Companion to the Supreme Court* (Oxford University Press, 1992), John A. Maltese, at p. 80.

7

Fundamental Rights and Judicial Review

I.

The question may be asked, What difference does it make whether a right is or is not held to be fundamental? Are not *all* rights, great or small, entitled to respect, protection, and vindication? Why should so much time and thought be given to differentiating fundamental from lesser rights?

Part of the answer to these questions has already been given in our previous discussion. We have seen that the Supreme Court has "incorporated" the Bill of Rights into the Fourteenth Amendment as a limit on State power, only "selectively"—only such rights as are deemed to be *fundamental* are guaranteed equally against State as against Federal encroachment; but rights, though enumerated in the Bill of Rights, considered not fundamental, remain as limitations *only* on the Federal Government.

Furthermore, once a right is found to be fundamental, it has the power to generate "penumbras, formed by emanations from these guarantees that help give them life and substance. . . . " Thus, e.g., the right of freedom of speech includes the right to distribute printed matter, the right to receive, the right to read, freedom of inquiry, freedom of thought, freedom to teach.[1] These rights are in a sense derivative from and ancillary to the right of freedom of speech, and yet they are not of a secondary or inferior rank; they are definitive of the very substance of the fundamental right guaranteed by the First Amendment. Rights that are not fundamental may not have this generative power.

Then, too, there are some rights which, though not specifically enumerated in the Constitution, are of such transcendent importance that their *fundamental* character must be judicially recognized and protected, such as the right to travel,[2] the right of parents to educate their child in a private rather than a public school,[3] and the right to study any subject or any foreign language.[4] While such rights may be put under the protection of the First Amendment or some other constitutional provision,[5] it would strain the language of the Constitution to stretch its words to include such rights—except, of course, the word "liberty" in the Due Process Clause in the Fifth and Fourteenth Amendments. By the term "liberty" the *fundamental* rights guaranteed by the Bill of Rights, as well as the penumbras formed by emanations from these guarantees, *and all other fundamental rights, whatever their source*, are—all of them—protected by the Constitution.

There are, then, some very important consequences that flow from denominating some rights as fundamental.

Justice Black vigorously and repeatedly attacked this constitutional development in all its aspects: (a) he urged incorporation of the entire Bill of Rights into the Fourteenth Amendment—an action which would have avoided differentiating some of the rights guaranteed by the Bill of Rights as fundamental; (b) he insisted on sticking to "the simple language" of the first eight amendments and not talk about some rights—e.g., the right of privacy—as emanations from one or more constitutional provisions; and (c) he questioned the reasoning in *Meyer* and *Pierce*, which was not anchored in the specific language of a provision of the Bill of Rights but seemed to place under constitutional protection rights not specifically enumerated in the Bill of Rights.[6] His arguments proved to be unpersuasive; they, however, served the purpose of displaying more clearly and definitively the steps taken by the Court in the development of the idea and role of fundamental rights.

II.

There is still another aspect of our inquiry which brings out the great importance of denominating some rights as fundamental—an aspect to which we now turn.

Judicial review of State laws is provided for by the Supremacy Clause (Art. VI), which states that the Constitution, the laws made in pursuance thereof, and the treaties of the United States, shall be the supreme law of the land, and that all State judges shall be bound thereby.

Whatever doubts may have existed with respect to the power of the Supreme Court to review and pass upon the constitutionality of congressional legislation, under the terms of Article III of the Constitution, they were effectively met by Chief Justice Marshall's opinion in *Marbury* v. *Madison*[7] in 1803, though dissenting voices are still heard.[8]

However, judicial review antedates the Constitution. Its function can be traced back to the common law, for certain principles of the common law, as Professor Corwin wrote,

> were earlier deemed to be "fundamental" and to comprise a "higher law" which even Parliament could not alter. "And it appears," wrote Chief Justice Coke in 1610, in his famous dictum in Bonham's case, "that when an act of Parliament is against common right and reason . . . The common law will control it and adjudge such act to be void." This idea first commended itself to Americans as offering an available weapon against the pretensions of Parliament in the agitation leading to the Revolution. Thus in 1765 the royal governor of Massachusetts Province wrote his government that the prevailing argument against the Stamp Act was that it contravened "Magna Charta and the natural rights of Englishmen and therefore, according to Lord Coke," was "null and void"; . . . In fact, the Cokian doctrine was invoked by the Supreme Court of the United States as late as 1874.[9]

Thus, the very idea of judicial review has its origin and basis in the doctrine that there are certain fundamental rights which no law may purport or attempt to contravene. Before the Bill of Rights was held applicable as a limitation on the States, the Supreme Court used natural law concepts or the idea of a "higher law"[10] as a depository of fundamental rights which limited the powers of States. Thus, e.g., the Court in 1874 in *Loan Association* v. *Topeka*[11] said:

> It must be conceded that there are . . . rights in every free government beyond the control of the State. There are limitations on [governmental] power which grow out of the essential nature of all free governments. Implied reservations of individual rights, without which the social compact could not exist, and which are respected by all governments entitled to the name.

Though the limitations may not be found in written constitutions, they are nonetheless in existence, are binding upon all branches of government, and are enforceable by the courts.

As we have related in an earlier chapter, however, beginning 1881,[12] litigants began to claim that fundamental rights were "privileges or immunities of citizens of the United States," protected against State action by the Fourteenth Amendment. While the Court rejected this contention, starting with *Gitlow*,[13] in 1925, the Court began the process of explicit "selective incorporation" of the Bill of Rights into the concept of "liberty" and the guarantee of "due process" of the Fourteenth Amendment. Thus, fundamental rights moved from the natural law or the doctrine of higher law to constitutional status, with "a local habitation and a name." And so, as can be clearly seen, the doctrine of fundamental rights and the doctrine of judicial review are inextricably intertwined through a long historical development that prominently includes the names of Lord Coke and of some of the leading builders of American constitutional law.

III.

Although judicial review is historically closely linked with the idea of fundamental rights, once the United States Constitution was ratified, Articles III and VI became the source of the Supreme Court's power to review and pass upon the constitutionality of State and Federal laws. Judicial review was not limited to statutes that allegedly contravened a provision of the Bill of Rights. *Marbury* v. *Madison*[14] involved no fundamental right. Marbury sought to compel Secretary of State Madison to deliver his commission which had been signed by President John Adams. The action was based on Sec. 13 of the Judiciary Act of 1789, which was interpreted to authorize the Court to issue writs of mandamus in suits falling within the Court's original jurisdiction. The Court held that Sec. 13 was unconstitutional as an attempt by Congress to expand the Court's original jurisdiction beyond what was provided by the Constitution. In 1796, five years before *Marbury* v. *Madison*, the Court held invalid a State law that was in conflict with the terms of a treaty,[15] and in 1810 the Court held that a State law was void as contravening the Constitution.[16] None of these cases involved what would be thought of today a fundamental right. What had happened was that the United States Constitution had come to take the place of what had been thought of as fundamental rights recognized by a "higher law."

The displacement, however, was by no means total, as we have seen. Justices Strong, Miller, Field, Harlan, Moody, and others preferred to rest the power of judicial review on broader ground than the language of the Constitution; but in the twentieth century the reliance has been on the line of constitutional reasoning which Chief Justice Marshall had charted in *Marbury* v. *Madison*.

The contrast between these two approaches comes out starkly when we see, e.g., what Justice Miller said for the Court in 1875[17] and what Justice Douglas said for the Court in 1965.[18]

It must be conceded, wrote Justice Miller,

> that there are private rights in every free government beyond the control of the State. A government which recognized no such rights, which held the lives, the liberty and property of its citizens subject at all times to the absolute disposition and unlimited control of even the most democratic depository of power, is after all but a despotism. It is true it is a despotism of the many, of the majority, if you choose to call it so, but it is none the less a despotism . . .
>
> The theory of our governments, state and national, is opposed to the deposit of unlimited power anywhere. . . .

When the Court had before it a Connecticut statute that made the use of contraceptives, even by a married couple, a criminal offense, Justice Douglas, writing for the Court, found that the case concerned "a relationship lying within the zone of privacy created by several fundamental constitutional guarantees," and he cited the "right of association contained in the penumbra of the First Amendment," the Third Amendment prohibition against the quartering of soldiers in any house in peacetime, the Fourth Amendment guarantee against unreasonable searches and seizures, the Fifth Amendment guarantee against compulsory self-incrimination, and the Ninth Amendment.

Justice Black, dissenting, had no difficulty in arguing that the opinion for the Court had been written for blind guides who strained at a gnat and swallowed a camel.[19] But he would have rejected Justice Miller's approach with at least equal vehemence. He wanted to stick to "the simple language of the Bill of Rights," in which he was unable to find a right of privacy.

IV.

Assuming the power of judicial review, how should the Court go about the business of testing a statute or other governmental action against the words of the Constitution? With respect to this question, the principles and doctrines were developed in different steps, under a variety of social and political pressures. The Court at no time worked out a comprehensive, consistent, clearly articulated set of principles; and to attempt here a history of the different steps would be tiresome and would divert us from our central interest, which is focused on the idea of fundamental rights.

Looking at the development retrospectively, the main lines without regard to chronology, seem to be the following principles or rules:

1. Legislative acts come before the Court with a presumption of constitutionality in their favor. In a case decided in 1969 Chief Justice Warren stated the principle in these words:

> Legislatures are presumed to have acted constitutionally even if source materials normally resorted to for ascertaining their grounds for action are otherwise silent, and their statutory classifications will be set aside only if no grounds can be conceived to justify them.[20]

This presumption obtains in both equal protection and due process cases.[21]

2. One who assails a statute as unconstitutional has the burden of showing that it does not rest upon any reasonable basis but is essentially arbitrary.[22] But a statute will not be set aside "if any state of facts reasonably may be conceived to justify it."[23]

3. These principles of judicial deference and self-restraint apply to statutes which regulate economic or social matters, but apply with far less force to laws that affect fundamental rights. When a statute deals with what is a legitimate legislative concern, but in a way that imposes a substantial burden on a fundamental right, the statute will be held to be unconstitutional; for the legislature must achieve its goal by means which have a "less drastic" impact on the fundamental rights.[24] Laws which actually affect the exercise of fundamental rights will not be sustained merely "because they were enacted for the purpose of dealing with some evil within the State's legislative competence, or even because the laws do in fact provide a helpful means of dealing with such an evil."[25]

V.

At this point in our discussion it becomes important to discuss the famous footnote 4 in the *Carolene Products* case[26] by Justice Stone. The case involved legislation affecting the sale of products "in imitation or semblance" of milk or cream. Concerning such legislation, said

Justice Stone, the Court will presume the existence of facts supporting the legislative judgment,

> for regulatory legislation affecting ordinary commercial transactions is not to be pronounced unconstitutional unless in the light of the facts made known or generally assumed it [i.e., the legislation] is of such a character as to preclude the assumption that it rests upon some rational basis within the knowledge and experience of the legislators.

At this point the opinion has footnote 4.[27] It states that

> There may be narrower scope for operation of the presumption of constitutionality when legislation appears on its face to be within a specific prohibition of the Constitution, such as those of the first ten amendments, which are deemed equally specific when held to be embraced within the Fourteenth. . . .
>
> It is unnecessary to consider now whether legislation which restricts those political processes which can ordinarily be expected to bring about repeal of undesirable legislation, is to be subjected to more exacting judicial scrutiny under the general prohibitions of the Fourteenth Amendment than are most other types of legislation. [Then the footnote cites cases that passed on restrictions upon the right to vote or upon the dissemination of information, interferences with political organizations, prohibition of peaceable assembly, statutes directed at particular religions, or national or racial minorities:] whether prejudice against discrete and insular minorities may be a special condition, which tends seriously to curtail the operation of those political processes ordinarily to be relied upon to protect minorities, and which may call for a correspondingly more searching judicial inquiry. . . .

The footnote strongly suggested that while the general rule is that the Court is to presume the constitutionality of legislation, a "more exacting judicial scrutiny"—a "more searching judicial inquiry"—may be necessary in two classes of situations: (a) when the legislation affects a fundamental right, such as the rights guaranteed by the Bill of Rights, and (b) when the legislation affects a racial, national (ethnic), or religious minority—"prejudice against discrete and insular minorities."[28]

The *Carolene* footnote 4 was written in a case decided in 1938—the year following the Court's decision in *West Coast Hotel* v. *Parrish*,[29] in which the Court in effect revised a decision it had made in the previous year,[30] and upheld a minimum wage statute. Thus, as can be readily seen, Justice Stone's footnote took on special significance because of its timing, for it came just as the Court had begun to move away from the "*Allgeyer-Lochner-Adair-Coppage* constitutional doctrine."[31] Although the footnote was not germane to the decision in *Carolene*, in a prescient way it charted the course of future significant constitutional development by distinguishing three basic types of legislation subject to judicial review—(a) statutes in the sphere of socioeconomic regulation, (b) statutes affecting fundamental rights, and (c) statutes affecting a racial, ethnic, or religious minority—and suggested different levels of intensity of judicial review.

By 1949 the Court had practically—though not theoretically—given up judicial review of social and economic legislation.[32] What the Stone footnote accomplished was that it signaled to the Court and the nation that the judicial abdication would not—could not—be total. The footnote in effect said that the constitutional turnabout which the Court had made only some months before would have no effect on the process of judicial review of legislation affecting fundamental rights or the rights of "discrete and insular minorities." The historical importance of Justice Stone's footnote can hardly be exaggerated. Its timing and its phrasing were masterful.

Four years after *Carolene*—in 1942—Stone, by then Chief Justice, first spoke of certain freedoms as having "a preferred position" in the Constitution. In *Jones* v. *Opelika*,[33] a case that involved freedom of speech and religion, Chief Justice Stone wrote that the Constitution, "by virtue of the First and Fourteenth Amendments, has put [freedom of speech and freedom of religion] in a preferred position." The phrase "preferred position," found its way into subsequent Court opinions dealing with First Amendment rights.[34] In more recent cases, however, it has been replaced by the older phrase, *fundamental rights*, which we have traced back to Justice Washington's opinion in *Corfield*.

Justice Frankfurter did not like the phrase "preferred position," nor did he approve of footnote 4,[35] because they suggested to him that legislation affecting First Amendment freedoms is "presumptively unconstitutional." But Justice Stone had made no such claim. He said only that certain kinds of statutes should be subjected to more rigorous judicial review than will be the case with legislation affecting only economic or social matters. The constitutional history since Justice Frankfurter's misdirected strictures have fully vindicated Justice Stone.

In the 1960s the Supreme Court, under Chief Justice Warren,[36] sharpened the footnote 4 analysis by combining into one the two types of situations in which strict scrutiny is indicated, so that the result was a "two-tier" approach, as follows:

(a) *The "reasonable basis" standard of judicial review*, under which the Court in effect defers to the legislative judgment on questions of economic relations and related matters. The legislative freedom involved in this standard of judicial review is well expressed in the following four-fold formula enunciated by the Court:[37]

1. The equal protection clause of the Fourteenth Amendment does not take from the State the power to classify in the adoption of police laws, but admits of the exercise of a wide scope of discretion in that regard, and avoids what is done only when it is without any reasonable basis and therefore is purely arbitrary.
2. A classification having some reasonable basis does not offend against that clause merely because it is not made with mathematical nicety or because in practice it results in some inequality.
3. When the classification in such a law is called in question, if any state of facts reasonably can be conceived that would sustain it, the existence of that state of facts at the time the law was enacted must be assumed.
4. One who assails the classification in such a law must carry the burden of showing that it does not rest upon any reasonable basis, but is essentially arbitrary.

This rule of "minimal scrutiny" has made it improbable that any governmental regulation in the socioeconomic sphere would be held unconstitutional, as a violation of due process or equal protection, yet it is important to note that

> even when deferring to legislative actions, the Court continually pointed to reasons that could justify such actions in terms of the general public interest, and explained why the legislation under review could be viewed as "an exercise of judgment" rather than "a display of arbitrary power."[38]

(b) *The "strict scrutiny" standard of judicial review*, of legislation affecting "fundamental interests" or a "discrete and insular" minority, i.e., a "suspect" classification. This type of judicial review has often been referred to as the *"compelling interest"* doctrine, by which is meant that the legislation comes before the Court with no or little presumption of constitutionality, and that the government must establish a high degree of need for the legislation; and this is the case "whether the impinging law be a classification statute to be tested against the Equal Protection Clause, or a state or federal regulatory law, to be tested against the Due Process Clause of the Fourteenth or Fifth Amendment."[39]

In his important dissenting opinion in *Shapiro* v. *Thompson*[40] Justice Harlan called attention to the fact that the "compelling interest" doctrine has a two-fold application, as follows: (a) to statutes which base classifications upon "suspect" criteria, and (b) to statutes which set up classifications that affect a "fundamental right."

Regarding the former, Justice Harlan found that racial classifications, "at least since" *Korematsu* v. *United States*,[41] have been regarded as inherently "suspect." In *Korematsu*, World War II Japanese exclusion case, Justice Black said for the Court that all legal restrictions

> which curtail the civil rights of a single racial group are immediately suspect. That is not to say that all such restrictions are unconstitutional. It is to say that courts must subject them to the most rigid scrutiny. Pressing public necessity may sometimes justify the existence of such restrictions; racial antagonism never can . . .

The latter branch of the "compelling interest" principle, Justice Harlan said, was first foreshadowed in *Skinner* v. *Oklahoma*,[42] in which the Court invalidated a State statute that provided for the compulsory sterilization of "habitual criminals." In his opinion for the Court, Justice Douglas said that the statute dealt with "one of the basic civil rights of man," since marriage and procreation "are fundamental to the very existence and survival of the race." The Court held that this being the case, the statute required "strict scrutiny."

Skinner was decided in 1942 and *Korematsu* in 1944, and so it is from those dates on that the "strict scrutiny" formulation has developed. With respect to its application to statutes involving fundamental rights, the formula reappeared in the apportionment case of *Reynolds* v. *Sims*[43] in 1964, and in voting rights cases in 1965 and 1966.[44] It was thus in the 1960s that the formula can be said to have become firmly fixed.

VII.

We have stated that the "compelling interest" doctrine—or the "strict scrutiny" rule—has a two-fold aspect in that it is applicable to statutes which base classifications upon "suspect" criteria, such as race, and to statutes which use classifications that affect a "fundamental right." It should be noted, however, that often it is difficult to say definitively that the Court's analysis plants the rationale in one category rather than the other; for sometimes a "fundamental interest" is at stake, and also a "suspect" classification is used or affected. Justice Harlan called attention to this problem in his dissenting opinion in *Shapiro*.

In that case, decided in 1969, the Court had before it statutes of two states, and an act of Congress applicable to the District of Columbia, under which welfare assistance was denied to persons who had not resided within their jurisdictions for at least one year. The Court, using the compelling interest test, held these acts unconstitutional as an impingement upon the affected persons' constitutional right to travel freely from state to state. As read by Justice Harlan, the majority opinion by Justice Brennan held as "suspect" a classification of persons based upon their interstate travel—those who had and those who had not moved from one state to another within the year. The majority opinion, according to Justice Harlan, also held as "suspect" a classification which differentiated persons who had exercised *a constitutional right* from those who had not done so, for the Court had said that in moving, the affected persons

> were exercising a constitutional right, and any classification which serves to penalize the exercise of that right, unless shown to be necessary to promote a *compelling* governmental interest, is unconstitutional. (Italics in original.)

Thus the statutes were "suspect" because of their invidious classifications. But they were "suspect" also for the reason that the classifications "touched on the fundamental right of interstate movement," for this is what the majority opinion said:

> Since the classification here touches on the fundamental right of interstate movement, its constitutionality must be judged by the stricter standard of whether it promotes a *compelling* state interest. (Italics in original.)

Two years later, in 1971, the Court[45] in an opinion by Justice Blackmun, tried to remove this ambivalence or these alternative readings by stating that the classification involved in *Shapiro*

> was subjected to strict scrutiny under the compelling state interest test, not because it was based on any suspect criterion such as race, nationality, or alienage, but because it impinged upon the fundamental right of interstate movement.

While this interpretation of the rationale of *Shapiro* by the Court itself may remove the ambiguity from that case, Justice Harlan was, on the whole, right in pointing to the fact that the two types of "compelling interest" situations are not always watertight, mutually exclusive. Analytically, however, it is helpful to follow Justice Stone's approach in footnote 4 of *Carolene* by considering a statute as either affecting a fundamental right or as affecting prejudicially a "discrete and insular" minority. There are difficulties enough inherent in either class of case without mixing them—though philosophically it must be admitted that "the notion of invidious classification . . . shares a close and complex relationship with notions of fundamental rights."[46]

Notes

1. *Griswold* v. *Connecticut*, 381 U.S. 479 (1965).
2. *Shapiro* v. *Thompson*, 394 U.S. 618 (1969).
3. *Pierce* v. *Society of Sisters*, 268 U.S. 510 (1925).
4. *Meyer* v. *Nebraska*, 262 U.S. 390 (1923).
5. See Justice Douglas in his opinion in *Griswold*; Justice Goldberg in *Aptheker* v. *Secretary of State*, 378 U.S. 500 (1964); and *United States* v. *Guest*, 383 U.S. 745 (1966).
6. Justice Black's dissenting opinion in *Griswold* v. *Connecticut*, 381 U.S. 479 (1965); also *Duncan* v. *Louisiana*, 391 U.S. 145 (1968).
7. *Marbury* v. *Madison*, 1 Cr. 137 (1803).
8. The literature in the judicial review controversy is extensive. See L. Lusky, *By What Right?* (1975); B. Berger, *Government by Judiciary* (1977); L. Krieger, *An Essay on the Theory of Enlightened Despotism* (1978); L. Hand, *The Bill of Rights* (1958); L. Boudin, *Government by Judiciary* (1932).
9. E. S. Corwin, *The Constitution and What It Means Today* (1978 ed.), 221–222.
10. C. G. Haines, *The Revival of Natural Law Concepts* (1930); B. Wright, *American Interpretations of Natural Law* (1931).
11. *Loan Association* v. *Topeka*, 87 U.S. 655 (1874), opinion by Justice Miller for the Court.
12. *Spies* v. *Illinois*, 123 U.S. 131 (1887).
13. *Gitlow* v. *New York*, 268 U.S. 652 (1925).
14. Note 7, supra.
15. *Ware* v. *Hylton*, 3 U.S. 199 (1796).
16. *Fletcher* v. *Peck*, 10 U.S. 87 (1810).
17. Case cited in note 11, supra.
18. Case cited in note 1, supra.
19. Matthew 23:24
20. *McDonald* v. *Board of Elections*, 394 U.S. 802 (1969).
21. This general, basic principle was stated by Chief Justice Marshall in *Fletcher* v. *Peck*, cited in note 16 supra.
22. *Lindsley* v. *Natural Carbonic Gas Co.*, 220 U.S. 61 (1911).
23. *McGowan* v. *Maryland*, 366 U.S. 420 (1961).
24. *U.S.* v. *Robel*, 389 U.S. 258 (1967).
25. *United Mine Workers* v. *Illinois Bar Assoc.*, 389 U.S. 217 (1967).
26. *U.S.* v. *Carolene Products Co.*, 304 U.S. 144 (1938).
27. For history of the preparation of this footnote, see A. T. Mason, *Harlan Fiske Stone* (1956), 512–515.
28. For Justice Frankfurter's critical discussion of the footnote, see *Kovacs* v. *Cooper*, 336 U.S. 77 (1949).

29. *West Coast Hotel v.* Parrish, 300 U.S. 379 (1937).

30. *Morehead* v. *New York ex rel. Tipaldo*, 298 U.S. 587 (1936).

31. *Lincoln Federal Labor Union* v. *Northwestern Iron and Metal Co.*, 335 U.S. 525 (1949).

32. But cf. *Philadelphia* v. *New Jersey*, 437 U.S. 617 (1978), in which, by 7–2 vote, the Court held that a state law prohibiting importation into the state of solid or liquid waste for disposal at landfills violates the Commerce Clause. But the statement in our text may be true without exception when one considers only cases that involved judicial review under due process or equal protection.

33. *Jones* v. *Opelika*, 316 U.S. 584 (1942), Stone's dissenting opinion at p. 608.

34. See citations in Justice Frankfurter's concurring opinion in *Kovacs* v. *Cooper*, 336 U.S. 77 (1949), at 93.

35. Case cited in note 34 supra.

36. Chief Justice Warren resigned in 1969.

37. *Morey* v. *Doud*, 354 U.S. 457 (1957), quoting from *Lindsley v. Natural Carbonic Gas Co.*, 220 U.S. 61 (1911).

38. Tribe, L. H., *American Constitutional Law* (1978), 451.

39. Justice Stewart, concurring opinion, *Shapiro* v. *Thompson*, 394 U.S. 618 (1969).

40. *Ibid.*

41. *Korematsu* v. *United States*, 323 U.S. 214 (1944).

42. *Skinner* v. *Oklahoma*, 316 U.S. 535 (1942).

43. *Reynolds* v. *Sims*, 377 U.S. 533 (1964).

44. *Carrington* v. *Rash*, 380 U.S. 89 (1965); *Harper* v. *Virginia Board of Elections*, 383 U.S. 663 (1966).

45. *Graham* v. *Richardson*, 403 U.S. 365 (1971).

46. Tribe, *op. cit.* supra note 38, at p. 1002.

8

Conclusion

I.

The doctrine of fundamental rights and the doctrine or rule of strict scrutiny did not arise simultaneously. Their interdependence may have been assumed but was not explicitly articulated before *Carolene's* footnote 4 in 1938; for example, in *Meyer* or *Pierce* there is no mention or even suggestion of the rule of strict scrutiny of the type of legislation involved in those cases. With the advantage of hindsight, however, it is reasonable to assimilate to the rule decisions that pre-date *Carolene*, and consider them as precedents for the rule, precisely as Justice Stone himself did in his footnote 4.

Looking, then, before and after, we find that the following rights, guaranteed by the Bill of Rights, are of a fundamental nature, and are, therefore, protected by the strict scrutiny rule in cases involving judicial review of Federal or State legislation:[1]

freedom of speech[2]
freedom of press[3]
freedom of assembly[4]
freedom of association[5]
freedom of petition[6]
freedom of religion[7]
separation of church and state[8]
guarantee against taking of private property without just compensation.[9]

Insofar as concerns limits on powers of the States, the foregoing are fundamental rights which may be said to be instances of substantive due process, or explications of the meaning of "liberty" as guaranteed by the Fourteenth Amendment.

While it cannot be said that for each of these rights a case can be cited that explicitly identifies it as a fundamental right, all of them have been held to be guarantees against the States, and hence selectively incorporated into the Due Process Clause of the Fourteenth Amendment. But since only rights considered to be fundamental are selected for such incorporation, all of them are, therefore, fundamental rights protected by the strict scrutiny rule.

By a similar line of reasoning, the following procedural rights, guaranteed by the Bill of Rights, are fundamental rights protected by the rule of strict scrutiny:

> guarantee against unreasonable search and seizure[10]
> guarantee against compulsory self-incrimination[11]
> guarantee against double jeopardy[12]
> right to counsel[13]
> right to a speedy trial[14]
> right to trial by jury[15]
> right to be confronted by witnesses[16]
> right to have compulsory process for obtaining witnesses[17]
> right to be free of cruel and unusual punishment[18]

Other rights recognized as fundamental—and therefore protected by the rule of strict scrutiny—are the following:

> right to reproduce; right not to be sterilized[19]
> right to privacy; right to prevent conception;[20] right to possess obscene material in privacy of one's home[21]
> right to teach and right to study; right to marry and bring up one's children according to one's own beliefs; right to conduct and right to attend private school.[22]
> right to travel[23]
> right to vote—"one person, one vote."[24]
> right of a woman to decide whether or not to terminate her pregnancy, but this is doubtful since *Casey*.[25]

When asked what has been the most significant, the most influential development in American constitutional law in the twentieth century, some would undoubtedly choose the school desegregation case, *Brown v. Board of Education*;[26] some would agree with Chief Justice Warren in pointing to the reapportionment cases of the 1960s.[27] Compelling reasons can be given for each of these choices. I submit, however, that the development with the widest and deepest reach has been that which has been discussed in this work, for it has been a development that has nationalized the Bill of Rights, that has moved the Bill of Rights, together with the Fourteenth Amendment, to the forefront of our consciousness, that has made civil liberties, civil rights, and human rights matters of prime concern, individually and institutionally. It has brought new life and vision to the Federal and State governments, to the thousands of courts of law throughout the country, and especially to the United States Supreme Court. This has been an achievement that is beyond the possibility of measurement.

The distance that we have traveled can be seen when we recall that in a case before the Supreme Court in 1908 it was said that the right to impart instruction, harmless in itself or beneficial to those who receive it, is a substantial right of *property*.[28] Today such a declaration would be considered shocking and would produce wide protests. We have come a long way, indeed.

Yes, we have come a long way, and both the process and the end result are gains of which Americans may justly be proud. It would, however, be Pollyannaish to disregard and be indifferent to the fact that there are forces and pressures that threaten what has been accomplished. For example, in a case decided in 1994, Justice Scalia, in a concurring opinion in a case that involved prosecution allegedly without probable cause, said:

> Except insofar as our decisions have included within the Fourteenth Amendment certain explicit substantive protections of the Bill of Rights—an extension I accept because it is both long established and narrowly limited—I reject the proposition that the Due Process Clause guarantees certain (unspecified) liberties, rather than merely guarantees certain procedures as a prerequisite to deprivation of liberty.[29]

In a case decided in 1993, Justice Scalia wrote in a concurring opinion, in which he was joined by Justice Thomas:

> I am willing to accept the proposition that the Due Process Clause of the Fourteenth Amendment, despite its textual limitation to procedure, incorporates certain substantive guarantees specified in the Bill of Rights; but I do not accept the proposition that it is the secret repository of all sorts of other, unenumerated, substantive rights—however fashionable that proposition may have been [in the *Lochner* era].[30]

And these are not voices crying in the wilderness. They have support, in varying degrees, in the Court itself, in the legal profession, in law schools, and in American society. Respect for precedent does not stand in the way to undoing well-established decisions or principles. This was made explicitly clear by Chief Justice Rehnquist in his dissenting opinion in *Casey* (in which he was joined by Justices Scalia, White, and Thomas). He wrote:

> In our view, authentic principles of stare decisis do not require that any portion of the reasoning in *Roe* be kept intact. "Stare decisis is not . . . a universal, inexorable command," especially in cases involving the interpretation of the Federal Constitution. . . . It is therefore our duty to reconsider constitutional interpretations that "depart from a proper understanding" of the Constitution.

Perhaps Justices of the Supreme Court ought to be warned, as St. Paul warned the Ephesians, not any longer to be children, "tossed to and fro and carried about with every wind of doctrine."[31]

Justice Black took satisfaction in claiming that he always carried in his pocket a copy of the Constitution. He attached to the Constitution the fervor that the Bible commands the people of Israel to have towards the Torah: its words "shall be upon thine heart; and thou shalt teach them diligently unto thy children, and shalt talk of them when thou sittest in thine house, and when thou walkest by the way, and when thou liest down, and when thou risest up."[32] Since, said Justice Black, he could not find the word "privacy" in the text, then there is no fundamental right of privacy. Justice Black's simplistic view of judicial review reminds one of what Justice Roberts said: When an act of the legislature is challenged as unconstitutional, the Court "has only one duty—to lay the article of the Constitution which is involved beside the statute which is challenged and to decide whether the latter squares with the former."[33] To do this, it seems, one hardly needed to go to college, let alone to a law school. If the process is so simple, how does one account for the fact that by 1995 there were already over five hundred volumes of Supreme Court Reports?

Sometimes this point of view is presented as the "original intent" philosophy or doctrine, with the claim that that intent is best discovered in the words, in the text of the Constitution.[34] A true view of the original intent of the Framers is, however, to be found in the philosophy of natural law and natural rights as expressed in the Declaration of Independence, and in the opinions in *Corfield* and in opinions of Justice Field, the first Justice Harlan, and others that we have considered.

These Justices—and James Madison, Thomas Jefferson—would not have asked—as was asked, in one set of words or another, by Justice Black, by Justices White, Rehnquist, Scalia, Thomas, by Judge Robert Bork—"Where in the Constitution do we find the fundamental right of privacy?" but instead would have asked, "Where in the Constitution is the power vested in the Congress or in the States to ban the use of contraceptives?"

In construing the Fourteenth Amendment, however, the ultimate consideration ought not to be history, nor tradition, nor precedent, although we may learn from such resources, but a constitutional theory or philosophy that places primary emphasis on an individual's right to be different, his or her fundamental right to "liberty," fundamental right to be let alone. "We are not," Justice Brennan has said, "an assimilative, homogeneous society, but a facilitative, pluralistic one, in which we must be willing to abide someone else's unfamiliar or even repellent practice because the same tolerant impulse protects our own idiosyncrasies . . . In a community such as ours, 'liberty' must include the freedom not to conform." We should not, he said, squash a person's freedom "by requiring specific approval from history before protecting anything in the name of liberty."[35]

In the last analysis, it *is*, indeed, the text of the Constitution that matters, and the text calls for "liberty," a word that the Framers, in 1789 and 1868, left undefined, left to the Court to define and apply. The nature of the word calls for a liberality of mind and spirit. To read it grudgingly, as if doing so under protest, is to forswear one's judicial duty. "The meaning of 'due process' and the content of terms like 'liberty,'" Justice Frankfurter wrote, "are not revealed by the Constitution. It is the Justices who make the meaning."[36] The words are largely empty of meaning. But they are words written into a *constitution*, a charter, a covenant, written to endure perpetually, for untold generations; the words must therefore be given life by minds that are attuned to the transcendent purpose for which the words were intended when written into a Constitution for a free-spirited society.

II.

As we have noted, in *Edwards* v. *California*, in 1941, the Supreme Court, relying on the Commerce Clause of Article I, invalidated a California statute that prohibited a person from bringing into the State any nonresident indigent person. The decision was unanimous. In a concurring opinion, however, Justice Jackson argued that the Court should hold that interstate travel is a privilege of national citizenship and that the statute violated the Privileges or Immunities Clause of the Fourteenth Amendment. This, he said, was the intent of the Citizenship and of the Privileges or Immunities Clauses of the Amendment. "But the hope proclaimed in such generality soon shriveled in the process of judicial interpretation. For nearly three-quarters of a century this Court rejected every plea to the privileges and immunities clause. . . . " More than a half-century after Jackson had written these words, in 1999 the Supreme Court resorted to the Privileges or Immunities Clause, in a case that had an affinity to *Edwards*. The case deserves our interest and discussion.

In 1992 California enacted a statute that limited the amount of welfare benefits for a family that had resided in California for less than twelve months to the amount that family would have received from the State of the family's prior residence. (California offered welfare benefits that were higher than those offered in forty-four other States.) In a class action, the Supreme Court, by vote of 7–2, held the statute to be unconstitutional.

In his opinion for the Court, Justice John Paul Stevens noted that although the word "travel" is not in the Constitution, yet the Court has held that the right to travel from one State to another is firmly embedded in the country's law; it is, he said, quoting from *Shapiro*, "a virtually unconditional personal right, guaranteed by the Constitution to us all." Justice Stevens defined the issue in the case as "the right of the newly arrived citizen to the same privileges and immunities [citing the Privileges and Immunities Clause of Article IV] enjoyed by other citizens of the same State. That right is protected not only by the new arrival's status as a State citizen, but also by her status as a citizen of the United States [citing the Citizen Clause and the Privileges or Immunities Clause of the Fourteenth Amendment]." Justice Stevens quoted with approval appropriate passages from the opinions of Justice Miller for the Court in the *Slaughter-House Cases* as well as from Justice Bradley's dissenting opinion in that case. The California statute should be subjected, the Court held, to the strictest scrutiny.

This case, *Saenz* v. *Roe*,[37] is notable not only for its decision and the Court's opinion, but also for the dissenting opinions. In his dissenting opinion, for himself and for Justice Clarence Thomas, Chief

Justice William H. Rehnquist stated that this case marked only the second time in the Court's entire history that life was breathed into the Privileges or Immunities Clause of the Fourteenth Amendment. Chief Justice Rehnquist noted that the California statute imposed no restriction on the right to enter the State; it, therefore, presents no issue of the traditional conception of the right to travel. Indeed, Chief Justice Rehnquist contended that the case did not at all involve the right to travel.

> If States can require individuals to reside in-state for a year before exercising the right to educational benefits, the right to terminate a marriage, or the right to vote in primary elections that all other state citizens enjoy, then States may surely do the same for welfare benefits. . . . Durational residence requirements were upheld when used to regulate the provision of higher education subsidies, and the same deference should be given in the case of welfare payments.

Justice Thomas, in his dissenting opinion, in which Chief Justice Rehnquist joined, noted that "the Court all but read the Privileges or Immunities Clause out of the Constitution in the *Slaughter-House Cases*" and that in his view "the majority [in *Saenz*] attributes a meaning to the Privileges or Immunities Clause that likely was unintended when the Fourteenth Amendment was enacted and ratified." Justice Thomas noted, with apparent disapproval, that *Slaughter-House* had held that "nearly every civil right . . . including those rights which are fundamental" are not protected by the Privileges or Immunities Clause of the Fourteenth Amendment. Reviewing the historical record of the adoption of the Fourteenth Amendment, Justice Thomas contended that its purpose was to adopt the reasoning of Justice Washington in *Corfield,* to give *constitutional support to all fundamental—but only fundamental—rights.* This is what he wrote: history "supports the inference that, at the time the Fourteenth Amendment was adopted, people understood that 'privileges or immunities of citizens' were fundamental rights, rather than every public benefit established by positive law." Welfare benefits are not fundamental rights but are, instead, a public benefit established by positive law, and are, therefore, outside the reach of the Privileges or Immunities Clause.

Concluding his dissenting opinion, Justice Thomas wrote:

> Although the majority appears to breathe new life into the Clause today, it fails to address its historical underpinnings or its place in our constitutional jurisprudence. Because I believe that the demise of the Privileges or Immunities Clause has contributed in no small part to the current disarray of our Fourteenth Amendment

jurisprudence, I would be open to reevaluating its meaning in an appropriate case. Before invoking the Clause, however, we should endeavor to understand what the framers of the Fourteenth Amendment thought that it meant. We should also consider whether the Clause should displace, rather than augment, portions of our equal protection and substantive due process jurisprudence. The majority's failure to consider these important questions raises the specter that the Privileges or Immunities Clause will become yet another convenient tool for inventing new rights limited solely by the "predilections of those who happen at the time to be Members of this Court."

Justice Thomas's belligerent opinion has, I believe, some support in the history of the adoption of the Fourteenth Amendment and in responsible jurisprudential reasoning, but few are listening, and the agenda he proposes comes too late. There is only a very slim chance that the revival of the Privileges or Immunities Clause by the Court will replace the roles played by the Due Process and the Equal Protection Clauses.

In the context of the study in which we are engaged, the most significant result of this case is that all members of the Court, in 1999, acknowledged that the Constitution gives special protection to rights that are *fundamental*, even when, as in the case of travel, the rights are not expressly enumerated in the Constitution. Whether mentioned or not in the Constitution, the "strict scrutiny" rule is intended to provide the largest degree of protection to fundamental rights.

Our study, beginning with *Corfield*, decided in 1823, and ending with *Saenz*, decided in 1999, has thus made a full circle, for both cases essentially involved the question what "Privileges," what "Immunities" are protected by the Constitution, and both cases found the answer in the concept of "fundamental" rights: that all—and only— fundamental rights are "Privileges" and "Immunities." Our study has shown that whether the Court considers the meaning of these constitutional words, or the meaning of the word "liberty" in the Due Process Clause, the real concern of the Court is with the proposition that the Constitution guarantees the *fundamental rights* of citizens, the rights that, in the words of Justice Cardozo, represent "the very essence of a scheme of ordered liberty . . . principles of justice so rooted in the traditions and conscience of our people as to be ranked as fundamental." Justices of the Supreme Court may differ as to what claimed rights meet the test, but, as we read the opinions in *Saenz*, the doctrine of fundamental rights stands firm and virtually impregnable.

Notes

1. Cf. list in Ch. IV, supra, used there for purpose of showing what rights have been selectively incorporated into the Fourteenth Amendment.
2. *Gitlow* v. *New York*, 268 U.S. 652 (1925).
3. *Near* v. *Minnesota*, 283 U.S. 697 (1931).
4. *Edwards* v. *South Carolina*, 372 U.S. 229 (1963).
5. *NAACP* v. *Alabama*, 357 U.S. 449 (1958).
6. *Edwards* v. *South Carolina*, 372 U.S. 229 (1963).
7. *Cantwell* v. *Connecticut*, 310 U.S. 296 (1940).
8. *Engel* v. *Vitale*, 370 U.S. 421 (1962).
9. *Chicago, B. & O. R. Co.* v. *Chicago*, 166 U.S. 226 (1897). But cf. *Dolan* v. *City of Tigard*, 129 L Ed 2d 304 (1994).
10. *Mapp* v. *Ohio*, 367 U.S. 643 (1961).
11. *Miranda* v. *Arizona*, 384 U.S. 436 (1966).
12. *Benton* v. *Maryland*, 395 U.S. 784 (1969).
13. *Gideon* v. *Wainwright*, 372 U.S. 335 (1963).
14. *Klopfer* v. *North Carolina*, 386 U.S. 213 (1967).
15. *In re Oliver*, 333 U.S. 257 (1948).
16. *Pointer* v. *Texas*, 380 U.S. 400 (1965).
17. *Washington* v. *Texas*, 388 U.S. 14 (1967).
18. *Furman* v. *Georgia*, 408 U.S. 238 (1972).
19. *Skinner* v. *Oklahoma*, 316 U.S. 535 (1942).
20. *Griswold* v. *Connecticut*, 381 U.S. 479 (1965); *Eisenstadt* v. *Baird*, 405 U.S. 438 (1972).
21. *Stanley* v. *Georgia,* 394 U.S. 557 (1969).
22. *Meyer* v. *Nebraska*, 262 U.S. 390 (1923); *Pierce* v. *Society of Sisters*, 268 U.S. 510 (1925); *Loving* v. *Virginia*, 338 U.S. 1 (1967).
23. *Shapiro* v. *Thompson*, 394 U.S. 618 (1969).
24. *Gray* v. *Sanders*, 372 U.S. 368 (1963); *Reynolds* v. *Sims*, 377 U.S. 533 (1964); *Baker* v. *Carr*, 369 U.S. 186 (1962).
25. *Roe* v. *Wade*, 410 U.S. 113 (1973) ; *Doe* v. *Bolton*, 410 U.S. 179 (1973). *Planned Parenthood* v. *Casey* 120 L Ed 2d 674 (1992).
26. *Brown* v. *Board of Education,* 347 U.S. 483 (1954).
27. *Baker* v. *Carr*, 369 U.S. 186 (1962); *Reynolds* v. *Sims*, 377 U.S. 533 (1964), the collective name of six cases.
28. *Berea College* v. *Kentucky*, 211 U.S. 45 (1908).
29. *Albright* v. *Oliver*, 127 L Ed 2d 114 (1994).
30. *TXO Production Corp.* v. *Alliance Resources Corp.*, 125 L Ed 2d 366 (1993.)
31. Ephesians IV:14.
32. Deuteronomy 6:4–9.
33. *U.S.* v. *Butler*, 297 U.S. 1, 62–63 (1936).
34. See Harry Jaffa, "Judge Bork's Mistake," *National Rev.* March 4, 1988.
35. *Michael H.* v. *Gerald D.*, 491 U.S. 110 (1989), dissenting opinion.
36. Felix Frankfurter, "The Supreme Court and the Public," *Forum.* June 1930.
37. *Saenz* v. *Roe*, 143 L Ed 2d 689 (1999).

Index of Cases

Index of Supreme Court Justices

Index